2006

THE BEST 10-MINUTE PLAYS
FOR TWO ACTORS

Smith and Kraus'
Short Plays and 10-Minute Plays Collections

Christopher Durang Vol. I: 27 Short Plays

Frank D. Gilroy Vol. II: 15 One-Act Plays

Israel Horovitz Vol. I: 16 Short Plays

Romulus Linney 17 Short Plays

Terrence McNally Vol. I: 15 Short Plays

Lanford Wilson: 21 Short Plays

Act One Festival 1995: The Complete One-Act Plays

Act One Festival 1994: The Complete One-Act Plays

EST Marathon 1999: The Complete One-Act Plays

EST Marathon 1998: The Complete One-Act Plays

EST Marathon 1997: The Complete One-Act Plays

EST Marathon 1996: The Complete One-Act Plays

EST Marathon 1995: The Complete One-Act Plays

EST Marathon 1994: The Complete One-Act Plays

HB Playwrights Short Play Festival

 2003 The Subway Plays

 2002 The Beach Plays

 2001 The Hospital Plays

 2000 The Funeral Plays

 1999 The Airport Plays

 1998 The Museum Plays

 1997 The Motel Plays

Twenty One-Acts from 20 Years at the Humana Festival 1975–1995

Women's Project and Productions Rowing to America & Sixteen Other Short Plays

8 TENS @ 8 Festival: 30 10-Minute Plays from the Santa Cruz Festivals I–VI

30 Ten-Minute Plays from the Actors Theatre of Louisville for 2 Actors

30 Ten-Minute Plays from the Actors Theatre of Louisville for 3 Actors

30 Ten-Minute Plays from the Actors Theatre of Louisville for 4, 5, and 6 Actors

2004: The Best 10-Minute Plays for Two Actors

2004: The Best 10-Minute Plays for Three or More Actors

2005: The Best 10-Minute Plays for Two Actors

2005: The Best 10-Minute Plays for Three or More Actors

2006: The Best 10-Minute Plays for Three or More Actors

2006
THE BEST 10-MINUTE PLAYS FOR TWO ACTORS

Edited by D. L. Lepidus

CONTEMPORARY PLAYWRIGHT SERIES

A Smith and Kraus Book
Hanover, New Hampshire

Published by Smith and Kraus, Inc.
177 Lyme Road, Hanover, NH 03755
www.SmithandKraus.com / (888) 282-2881

First Edition: December 2007
10 9 8 7 6 5 4 3 2 1

Manufactured in the United States of America
Cover and Text Design by Julia Hill Gignoux, Freedom Hill Design
Cover photo by Fred Marco. Josh Foldy and Stephanie Cozart in *The Proposal* by Stephen Bittrich, produced by The Drilling Company, directed by Carol Halstead.

ISBN-13 978-1-57525-563-7
ISSN 1550-6754
Library of Congress Control Number: 2007937063

Contents

Introduction

The ten-minute play as an accepted dramatic form is a fairly recent development. Some would say that its popularity is a result of our diminished attention spans, which may be partially true; but here's how the genre came to be.

For several years, Actors Theatre of Louisville, under the leadership of Jon Jory, commissioned playwrights to write plays of short duration for performance by its apprentice company. This was a way for the theater to do something to help playwrights, but also it was a way to develop relationships with them, many of which bore fruit over the years as these writers went on to have full-length plays staged in Actors Theater's famed Humana Festival.

Over the years, Actors Theatre built up quite a library of these short plays, all of them in manuscript. An editor for the play publisher Samuel French got the idea that maybe other theaters, actors, and students might be interested in these plays if they were made available to them. He managed to swing a deal for French to publish an anthology of Actors Theatre's best short plays, which they were now calling "ten-minute plays." This anthology was so successful that French has now published six such volumes, and most of the other publishers have followed suit, including Smith and Kraus, as its annual ten-minute plays anthologies will attest. Bills of ten-minute plays are now produced regularly — all over the world.

There are some who feel that the ten-minute play ought to be an opportunity for playwrights to experiment — with language, with form, with character, with subject matter. "The best" ten-minute plays are therefore the ones that depart the most from conventional drama. For the purposes of this series, here is how I define "best": that which is most useful to people who will buy this book and produce these plays. Some actors and directors prefer straightforward realism; whereas others go for more abstract, experimental plays. I don't carry a torch for any one style, so I have tried to include in this book examples of realism and, shall we say, "non-realism." I hope you will find herein more than one play that rings your bell. They all rang mine.

Should you find a play (or plays) in this book that you want to produce, you will find information in the back on who to contact for performance rights.

D. L. Lepidus
Brooklyn, N.Y.

PLAYS FOR
ONE MAN
AND
ONE WOMAN

The Proposal

STEPHEN BITTRICH

For Paula

The Proposal was first produced as a workshop production by The Drilling Company (www.drillingcompany.org), Hamilton Clancy, Artistic Director, along with seven other one-acts all on the theme of *Security* on June 9, 2006, at the 78th Street Theatre Lab, New York City. It was directed by Carol Halstead; Set Design by Rebecca Lord; Light Design by Miriam Crowe; Percussionist — Thom Garvey; Stage Manager — Billie Davis. It had the following cast: Julia Hightower — Stephanie Cozart; William Ainsworth — Josh Foldy.

CHARACTERS

JULIA HIGHTOWER: twenties, handsome and proud, talented in art, progressive in thought and action, but stuck in a time when a woman's role was limited to finding a husband.

WILLIAM AINSWORTH: mid- to late-thirtyish, proud and rakishly handsome, arrogant and rich. Ainsworth is a man accustomed to getting what he wants in the world.

Both characters must have upper class English accents.

SETTING

The sprawling grounds of Willowbrook Estate near Bishops Waltham in Hampshire, England, 1815.

• • •

At Rise: Julia Hightower, twenties, handsome and proud, but clearly distraught, paces about the garden. William Ainsworth, late thirtyish, proud and rakishly handsome, enters the lengthening evening shadows and observes her a moment before he speaks.

MR. AINSWORTH: There you are Miss Hightower. I was beginning to think I'd be called upon to fish you from the trout stream.

JULIA: Beg your pardon, I required a bit of air.

MR. AINSWORTH: Ah, yes. Lovely evening for it.

(Pause.)

And are you sufficiently pleased with the grounds of Willowbrook?

JULIA: Of course.

MR. AINSWORTH: Splendid — then you approve?

JULIA: Who could find fault with . . . *the grounds*, Mr. Ainsworth?

MR. AINSWORTH: No indeed. No indeed.

(Beat.)

But then I derive from your careful inflection that there is that at Willowbrook which you *could* find fault with, Miss Hightower.

JULIA: I — I cannot —

MR. AINSWORTH: Ah, tush, tush, not another word of it.

(Beat.)

Beautiful, clear night. Did you take in the full moon rising above the peat bogs?

JULIA: I marked it.

MR. AINSWORTH: Dramatic indeed.

(Pause.)

You know, Ms. Hightower, I rather blush to say, but the highlight of my trip to Sussex last summer was not the tedious family business which beckoned me thither, no, no, but rather my brief sojourn in Heathfield and the various social gatherings during which I was privileged to make the acquaintance of you and your family.

JULIA: *(With a taste of irony.)* It was a thrilling season.

MR. AINSWORTH: And during the picnic at Heathfield Park I must confess I was most smitten with your wonderful charcoal sketches of the countryside. It is thrilling indeed to discover a woman of such varied and studied accomplishment. Upon leaving there, I admit, I could think of not much else for sometime . . . but *you* . . . and your beautiful sketches.

JULIA: You flatter, Mr. Ainsworth.

MR. AINSWORTH: No, indeed, I do not. I very greatly wished to be . . . connected to you and your great talent — to have some ownership in it.

JULIA: Ownership?

MR. AINSWORTH: And when your family took lodgings in Hampshire this Spring it seemed a fortuitous event indeed.

JULIA: Quite fortuitous. I must return to the house, Mr. Ainsworth. It grows cold.

MR. AINSWORTH: Then let me warm you, Ms. Hightower . . . Julia.

JULIA: No —

MR. AINSWORTH: Please, take my coat.

JULIA: I fear the chill has deeply set in. There is no remedy you can provide.

MR. AINSWORTH: *(Relinquishing all false civility.)* I grow weary of these intrigues and double entendres. I am not a stupid man, Miss Hightower. I know the particulars for your family's visit. Plainly, your parents mean to parade you about polite society as a farmer at the county fair flaunts his choicest pig —

JULIA: Mr. Ainsworth!

MR. AINSWORTH: — but, and please excuse my audacious candor, you won't be winning any ribbons, I'm sorry to say, nor any husbands either for that matter, because, as sordid as it may be, there are scurrilous and unseemly tongues that wag this way and that 'round this tiny little hamlet. And they wag, Miss Hightower, about you.

(Julia appears almost dizzy from Mr. Ainsworth's utter lack of decorum.)

JULIA: I'm sure . . . I'm sure I haven't the faintest notion —

MR. AINSWORTH: You are a marked woman. There it is. Sorry to be the bearer of ill tidings. But there 'tis. You may as well sew your old maid's weeds forthwith because no suitors of any repute will be knocking at your door.

JULIA: How dare you, sir!

MR. AINSWORTH: I dare, Miss Hightower. I am the first-born son of the wealthiest man in Christendom. In all truthfulness, mere social convention is a paltry constraint for my sizeable wealth and stature. I dare . . . because I can. The fates, however, have been less kind to you. Being without a male sibling, your birthright, such that it is, has been entailed away, and your future, but for the unsecured and certainly meager offerings of an obscure male relative, can promise nothing more than abject poverty.

JULIA: *(After a beat, regaining her composure.)* And yet . . . I do not tremble, Mr. Ainsworth.

MR. AINSWORTH: *(After a beat, taking her in.)* And yet you do not. There is much to be admired in you, Julia.

JULIA: And much to be abhorred in you.

MR. AINSWORTH: And still . . . such an abhorred man as I might yet be your salvation.

(Beat.)

I like you, Julia.

JULIA: Mr. Ainsworth, you've said quite enough.

MR. AINSWORTH: Are you surprised? Yes, I like you. You are as handsome a specimen as ever I've seen, lively and energetic, talented in music and art, intelligent almost to a fault. These attributes, I daresay, when matched with my own myriad of graces, could well produce exceptionally pleasing offspring.

JULIA: Thank you for you astute observations, Mr. Ainsworth, but despite your previous reference to prized livestock, you'll be surprised to learn, I am no farm animal. Producing "exceptionally pleasing offspring" is not my life's chief objective.

MR. AINSWORTH: *(Ignoring and pressing on.)* Be assured, I am not looking for love, Julia, and I am quite certain that you do not love me. However, I do require a wife, a partner, in the business of expanding my honorable lineage. It is a grand, unbroken line spanning centuries before me, and I am called upon to bid adieu to the temptations and distractions of my youth and perform my family duty. I see you as a worthy candidate.

JULIA: Mr. Ainsworth, though your described partnership of convenience is no doubt brimming with fruitful promise, you will be shocked to discover your eloquent declaration of affection met with rejection. I hope the disappointment will not linger with you for long. Good evening, sir.

(She starts to leave, and He cuts her off.)

MR. AINSWORTH: Julia, certainly you are not ignorant of what I can offer a woman such as yourself in a "partnership of convenience" as you describe it. Not that I care a jot for social mores, but you cannot be completely unaware that your very reputation has recently been called into question. Your association with a local artist, a certain Monsieur Legard, whose name alone inspires credulity, is fatty meat for the maw of outrage, namely, the elder matrons of Bishops Waltham.

JULIA: My association with the gifted Mr. Legard is of my concern alone—

MR. AINSWORTH: Unjust, I know. Your guilt in this acquaintance, real or imagined, pure or impure, has set you alone and adrift at sea. And I alone am your last hope for security, Ms. Hightower.

JULIA: Really, Mr. Ainsworth, I think you missed your calling. Prize pigs, gristle-filled maws, adrift at sea. It seems you have a bent toward the poetic. But perhaps you should have said, "I alone might offer a sturdy mast and sail" . . . or "I alone am a fruitful uncharted isle in your course" or better still "I alone am the *God Poseidon* deigning to grant fair seas for your passage home."

MR. AINSWORTH: Perhaps I might have.

JULIA: Mr. Legard, whom, as you have intimated, is of French heritage is in fact as true an Englishman as you or I. He is my friend, and his skill with either brush or chisel is equal to anything I have seen displayed in the National Gallery. I admire his talent.

MR. AINSWORTH: Yes, I agree he is talented. I've seen his nudes. He's an eye for detail.

(She starts again to leave. He grabs her arm.)

JULIA: Mr. Ainsworth, you will let go my arm!

MR. AINSWORTH: *(Pulling her close.)* The deal is sealed, Ms. Hightower. Your parents have already accepted my offer of matrimony and despite social propricties dictating the contrary, have accepted a generous gift of real estate in this accord. You have been sold —

JULIA: — I will not bow —

MR. AINSWORTH: Nay, but you will! As I said, Miss Hightower. You have been sold. I possess the painting!

JULIA: *Wh-what did you say?*

MR. AINSWORTH: I possess the painting. And I think you must know the one I mean.

JULIA: Impossible . . .

MR. AINSWORTH: *(Quiet and vicious, in her ear.)* It did not come cheaply. *(Beat.)*
You now sit precariously on the edge of ruin. If you do not accept my

magnanimous offer, you will suffer the pangs of social ignominy that only an itinerant leper might endure. And moreover, I am quite certain that Mr. Legard will never in his short career see profit from a single painting in all of Hampshire. You *will* give me satisfaction.

(She crumbles to her knees and begins to cry. The Willowbrook Rectory bell tolls six times during the course of the following exchange.)

JULIA: Have you no heart? Have you no soul? I — I love him.

MR. AINSWORTH: I know.

(Beat.)

The rectory bell begs the question . . . will we be married?

JULIA: *(After a pause.)* Y-Yes.

(The lights fade to black.)

END OF PLAY

Don't Listen to
What It Sounds Like

Mark Borkowski

Don't Listen To What It Sounds Like was originally produced at Tribeca Lab in New York City under the direction of Randy Cherkas with the following cast: Floyd — Edmond Wilkinson; Gretchen — Laura Fay Lewis. More recently, *Don't Listen To What It Sounds Like* was produced at The American Globe Theatre in New York City under the direction of Robert Haufrecht with the following cast: Floyd — Chris Kerson; Gretchen — Suzette Azariah Gunn.

CHARACTERS
> FLOYD: thirties
> GRETCHEN: twenties

SETTING
> A modest apartment

TIME
> The present. Afternoon.

• • •

Lights Rise: Floyd is already ranting at Gretchen. She sits in a chair politely listening . . .

FLOYD: My blood flowing from open wounds. My body hanging from a barbed wire fence. My meat tearing from its thorns. Slipping onto the subway tracks and the subway car ravaging my body to pieces. Animals attacking me from all sides, ripping me apart. My tongue pulled out of my mouth. Decapitation. Castration. Fingers caught in table saws.

> My own personal apocalypse. Why am I haunted with these images?

GRETCHEN: It's . . . good to see you again, Floyd.

FLOYD: You asked me what was on my mind.

GRETCHEN: I asked you . . . how you were doing. I'm sorry.

FLOYD: Why are you sorry? What have you got to be sorry for? For asking me?

GRETCHEN: No, not at all.

FLOYD: Well, that's that. It's off my chest . . . for the moment. It's part of you now.

GRETCHEN: It's been a while.

FLOYD: Should be glad.

GRETCHEN: No.

FLOYD: Should count your lucky fucking stars —

GRETCHEN: I missed you.

FLOYD: Missed me ? You know what it's been like — what I had to go through since I last saw you ?

GRETCHEN: I'd like to know.

FLOYD: No you don't. I'm lucky I'm alive. Is that luck? Sometimes I wonder.

GRETCHEN: You look good.

FLOYD: Look, Gretch, you don't have to do that.

GRETCHEN: Do what ?

FLOYD: *You* look good.

GRETCHEN: I moved back.

FLOYD: Why?

GRETCHEN: Variety of reasons. My mother's sick.

FLOYD: Sounds like the main reason.

GRETCHEN: It's up there.

FLOYD: She's a good woman. She was always good to me. She always brought me something. She came to see you every day.

GRETCHEN: So did your mom.

FLOYD: Not every day. Christ, I been institutionalized so much the novelty wore off for her long before that.

GRETCHEN: She'd always bring cokes. You had a vanilla and I had —

FLOYD: Cherry coke. You hated vanilla.

GRETCHEN: Until I finally tried it.

FLOYD: Then you loved it.

GRETCHEN: I seem to be like that with everything.

FLOYD: Good woman, your mother.

GRETCHEN: In fact, I think I have some vanilla. I'm sure I have coke. I could make —

FLOYD: You really look good, Gretch.

GRETCHEN: I feel good.

FLOYD: Really. *(Pause, disappointed.)* That's good.
(Pause.)

GRETCHEN: Yeah, it's her heart. Mother always had problems with her heart.

FLOYD: She has a good heart, your mother.

GRETCHEN: Physically, I mean.

FLOYD: She was always good to me.

GRETCHEN: Can I offer you anything?

FLOYD: Your mind . . .

GRETCHEN: What ?

FLOYD: . . . it feels . . . OK ?

GRETCHEN: My mind ? It's a . . . nice place these days.

FLOYD: How did you do it ?

GRETCHEN: Do what ?

FLOYD: Get yourself together.

GRETCHEN: Time.

FLOYD: Time? Don't make me laugh.

GRETCHEN: Why?

FLOYD: Time. *(Facetiously.)* I don't know, maybe we have different concepts of time. Maybe there's no space in my time. Too crowded to move so therefore it doesn't move at all — because that's what it feels like!

GRETCHEN: Floyd —

FLOYD: We were in the same place at the same time. One equally as fucked up as the other. We were on the same medications.

GRETCHEN: We had different illnesses.

FLOYD: We were diagnosed with the same thing. That's how we bonded or don't you remember? Our illnesses brought us together. Time. I've been in and out of institutions for the past fifteen years. Have you?

(Pause, no response from her.)

Well, have you ?

GRETCHEN: No.

FLOYD: No. Still taking your medication? Answer me, are you? Or did they up it — did they up your dosage?

GRETCHEN: No, they didn't.

FLOYD: And why didn't they?

GRETCHEN: Because I'm not taking medication anymore.

FLOYD: Right. So then, tell me, how-did-you-do-it? Your mind's "such a nice place these days," such a Goddamn resort area —

GRETCHEN: Look, I'm sorry if you're upset —

FLOYD: I'm just talking loudly — I'm not as upset as I sound.

GRETCHEN: You sound like —

FLOYD: — what, I sound like what?

GRETCHEN: Like . . . you're upset, because . . .

FLOYD: Because why?

GRETCHEN: Because . . . I'm better.

FLOYD: That's not true.

GRETCHEN: That's what it sounds like.

FLOYD: Don't listen to what it sounds like!

GRETCHEN: What d'ya mean don't listen to —

FLOYD: Because I didn't mean it that way. My God, you even have that look on your face.

GRETCHEN: What look?

FLOYD: That they do.

GRETCHEN: Who? Who the hell are you talking about?

FLOYD: They'd have that look on their face — we use to imitate that look, we use to make fun of them. And now you got that look on your face, in your eyes, in the tone of your voice.

GRETCHEN: My voice?

FLOYD: That condescending voice.

GRETCHEN: I'm sorry, Floyd — I'm sorry you feel that —

FLOYD: What are you sorry for?

GRETCHEN: I'm allowed to be sorry! I'm allowed to be sorry for anything I wanna be sorry for!

FLOYD: I shouldn't be acting this way with you.

GRETCHEN: I understand.

FLOYD: You don't have to say that.

GRETCHEN: I'm not being condescending, I mean it — I understand. You think I don't remember how it feels?

FLOYD: Do you? Then why are you sorry? You have nothing to be sorry for. You look great, you sound great. Is that why you're sorry?

GRETCHEN: And I'm sorry I left.

FLOYD: Well . . .

GRETCHEN: And that I never wrote or called you . . .

FLOYD: Wherever you went . . . did you good. Maybe I should go there. Listen to me, as if there's actually a place you can fix things. Hotel Sanity. It's gotten really bad, Gretch. It's to the point where I can't go on a subway platform. I can't look at knives without my imagination using them. I see traffic I can't cross the street. Sometimes I run the other way. You know what it's like to not be able to cross the street? To stand there and watch old people, little kids, animals cross and there I am, paralyzed. Some days I can't even leave the house.

GRETCHEN: What does the doctor say?

FLOYD: He's sick of hearing it. You know how they get when you go on with something, over and over, for so long. They get bored, they look right through you.

GRETCHEN: I don't know what to say.

FLOYD: You always use to know what to say. You use to be so happy that somebody else felt the same way you did. We use to help each other.

GRETCHEN: God, I'm — I'm so removed from that state of mind then — then you'll say something and I'll . . . I'll remember. Like what you just said. How I use to get excited when we'd talk? I felt so much comfort knowing I wasn't the only one.

FLOYD: I miss that.

GRETCHEN: I'm afraid of the things you say.

FLOYD: You didn't use to be.

GRETCHEN: I've put it behind me. I never wanna go back there again.

FLOYD: You were slicing your wrists every other week.

GRETCHEN: Horizontally, not vertically.

FLOYD: They were always repainting your room.

GRETCHEN: I always conveniently missed my pulse.

FLOYD: You attempted it — you telling me you didn't?

GRETCHEN: It doesn't matter anymore.

FLOYD: For posterity sake.

GRETCHEN: Yes, I attempted it, but —

FLOYD: No buts! I don't wanna hear any buts! There are no buts! So . . . you don't see things anymore? 'Member the little people? They use to get into your head and tell you to do things?

GRETCHEN: I don't hear them anymore.

FLOYD: You still see the hands, right? The hands that would come out from under your bed?

GRETCHEN: They stopped.

FLOYD: You still forget to breathe?

GRETCHEN: No.

FLOYD: Sometimes you do, right?

GRETCHEN: Not at all.

FLOYD: Do you at least still make yourself throw up after you eat?

GRETCHEN: I'm sorry.

FLOYD: I remember how we use to comfort each other. Do you forget that too?

GRETCHEN: Of course not.

FLOYD: We were sick together.

GRETCHEN: 'Member how we thought we were aliens?

FLOYD: And we just couldn't fit.

GRETCHEN: I fit now, Floyd.

FLOYD: Despite how I'm behaving I'm . . . actually very happy for you.
(She hugs him.)

GRETCHEN: Let me make you that vanilla coke. We have a lot of catching up to do!
(Gretchen exits into the kitchen and fixes the drinks. Offstage.)
I hope I have vanilla. Yes! You're in luck. You know I drink these all the time now. Can't believe I was so stubborn, never trying it, as much as you bugged and bugged me. Then I finally try it and I'm addicted to it.
(At some point Floyd quietly exits. She continues talking, oblivious that he is gone.)
I swear, I'm like that with everything. Avocados. Yogurt. I'm like "no-no-no," then I can't stop eating it.
(She enters, carrying the vanilla cokes.)
When I think of how many things I hate that I never tried —
(She suddenly stops, wondering where he is.)
Floyd?

(She walks across the room, looking for him.)
Floyd?
(She stops, realizing he is gone. She sits, still holding the vanilla cokes.)
(Lights fade to black.)

END OF PLAY

Blue in the Face

KAYLA CAGAN

Blue in the Face was an Actor's Theater of Louisville Heideman Award Finalist in 2000. It was produced by Tex in the City in their 4 Your Consideration Art Series at the Gershwin Hotel, New York City, N.Y., directed by Meredith Lucio. Marion was played by Liz Wong and Andrew was played by Robert Sperlinga.

CHARACTERS

MARION: mid-twenties
ANDREW: mid-twenties

A couple recently split

TIME

Now

SETTING

New York City

AUTHOR'S NOTE

/ at the end of character's speech means that the character's speech should be interrupted by the next character's speech.

•   •   •

Andrew enters his former apartment. Marion throws keys at Andrew.

ANDREW: Well, if it isn't the patron saint of assholes.

MARION: Guess what I did today.

ANDREW: You sat and pondered your next great masterpiece.

MARION: Guess again.

ANDREW: Man, I never guess right. Hhmmm . . .

MARION: Never. You're not even close to warm.

ANDREW: Cold.

MARION: Colder.

ANDREW: Freezing.

MARION: You are an iceberg.

(Long pause.)

ANDREW: Thanks for the keys.

MARION: You're all set.

ANDREW: I appreciate you lending me *your* place.

MARION: *My* space.

ANDREW: You mind if I get a brewski?

MARION: Why should I mind now? I'll get it for you.

(She exits. As she re-enters, she holds the cans behind her back.)

Guess.

ANDREW: Right hand.

MARION: Guess again.

ANDREW: Other right hand.

MARION: Guess again.

ANDREW: Left foot.

MARION: Guess again.

(Andrew moves toward Marion. They are close to kissing, but don't.)

ANDREW: I don't think I need to guess anymore.

MARION: You never figured out what I did today.

(He takes the beer from her and begins to drink.)

ANDREW: (Sighs.) Did not.

MARION: So . . .

ANDREW: So.

MARION: Aren't you the least bit/

ANDREW: Why should I care what you do anymore? You kicked me out/

MARION: Out of the apartment/

ANDREW AND MARION: But not out of your/my life.

(Pause.)

MARION: I'll tell you what I did today.

ANDREW: I've got Beannie in the car, if this is going to be a while. I just came by to get the/

MARION: You have Beannie in the car? Why didn't you tell me? Why didn't you bring her in?

ANDREW: I didn't want to confuse her.

MARION: I'll bring her some water.

ANDREW: She has water, and her chew, and her bone. She's fine. You'll see her on the weekend.

MARION: I'm still her mommy.

ANDREW: No, you aren't. You are her "weekends only" mommy, her "only when things are fun" mommy. I'm the one who walks her every morning. I'm the one cleaning up her crap.

MARION: Yeah, I'm really glad she doesn't crap on Saturday and Sunday. That would suck.

ANDREW: Well, thanks for the keys and letting me use the place. I should be/

MARION: What? Before this turns ugly?

ANDREW: Thank God we were never married.

(Pause.)

MARION: Do you hate me yet?

ANDREW: How am I supposed to answer that?

MARION: Well, I have an answer for you.

(She raises her shirt to show off a new, swelling belly ring.)

How's this?

(She prances.)

ANDREW: Oh.

MARION: That's all you can say/

ANDREW: Yes.

MARION: I thought/

ANDREW: You thought what? I'd appreciate that/

MARION: I thought it would make you laugh.

ANDREW: For three years I asked you to get it pierced. Two months after we break up/

MARION: I finally followed your advice! Irony! Get it?!?!

ANDREW: You must be pleased.

MARION: No, I'm just a bitch.

ANDREW: Yes, you are.

(Pause.)

Can I touch it?

(She nods. He goes to her and touches her belly.)

MARION: Be careful! It hurts like hell. It stings. Your hands are cold!

ANDREW: It's turning blue, kind of pinkish blue/

MARION: A bruise.

ANDREW: So, why'd you do it? You want to tell me anyway, right, so . . .

MARION: Listen, I'm letting you borrow this place of *ours* and I'm letting you have the extra keys again, so/

ANDREW: *(He grabs her by the hips.)* What the hell is this, Marion?

(Long pause.)

MARION: Do you want to hear how it happened or don't you?

ANDREW: What choice do I have?

MARION: I didn't go to Bloomingdale's to get it done. I went to a little cosmetology school down in the Bowery. I thought it would they would be careful, clean, cautious, considerate/

ANDREW: Catatonic/

MARION: I was held down in this barber chair. My jeans were unbuttoned, my shirt was untied, and I felt four clumsy hands on me, all students, pushing and pulling my skin and then there was this little plastic gun. I told them I was changing my mind, I was frightened, there wasn't even any ice, I thought there would be ice/

ANDREW: You weren't, raped, you know/

MARION: I did this for you.

ANDREW: Did you rehearse this? You're really being weird.

(Marion stares at Andrew.)

MARION: I saw myself hanging upside down in a mirror on the wall behind the students. I turned blue for you. My eyes turned purple and my cheeks filled like plums and my lips were numb and cold and greenish and when I thought I was going to be sick/

(Marion runs to the sink and throws up. Andrew watches.)

MARION: I went cold.

ANDREW: Colder.

MARION: Freezing.

ANDREW: You were an iceberg.

MARION: I went numb because of you, I went cold, I went blue/

ANDREW: But you are here now. And your stomach looks so . . .

MARION: I don't feel well.

ANDREW: Let me see your stomach again.

MARION: Be careful.

(She lifts her shirt.)

ANDREW: For Christ's sakes, Marion, it's turning gray.

MARION: They said I had to clean it with peroxide twice daily, like when you get your ears pierced.

ANDREW: I've never had my ears pierced/

MARION: Not now, please.

ANDREW: You need to get this thing out of you. Go in the bathroom and get a cold rag/

MARION: It's fucking Florence Nightingale!

ANDREW: I'm trying to help you! I'm not the one puking my guts out while my abdomen is bloating into the Good Year Blimp. Now shut your mouth and help me!

MARION: No fucking way.

ANDREW: Same old Marion/

MARION: I want it now! I'm not taking it out/

ANDREW: Yeah, Marion, you are/

MARION: No, I'm not/

(Andrew grabs Marion and throws her on the couch. He straddles her, trying to pin her down so that he can reach her stomach without a fight. Marion scratches him.)

ANDREW: Let me/

MARION: Get your hands/

ANDREW: What? What is it? WHAT THE HELL DO YOU WANT, MARI-ON?

(Andrew gets off of her. They sit on the couch, panting.)

ANDREW: I came to get the keys. That's all I wanted.

MARION: Well, you got what you wanted the minute you walked in the door. Why did you stay?

ANDREW: Why do I always stay, Marion?

MARION: You should go.

ANDREW: I should.

(Pause.)

ANDREW: Beannie needs me. Beannie is out in the car.

MARION: I know she is/

ANDREW: I'm sorry you are so/

MARION: Cold?

ANDREW: I'll bring Beannie by on/

ANDREW AND MARION: Friday.

(Andrew takes one last sip of beer and exits. Marion picks up her beer, takes a swig. She starts to pull at her ring, but it hurts too much. She lightly taps the can against her belly, softly repeating "Cold, colder, freezing, iceberg." Lights fade as Marion passes out on the couch.)

END OF PLAY

Double D

JIM DALGLISH

Spring Playwright's Festival, The Provincetown Theater
Company, Provincetown, Mass., March 14, 2004. 2006 Turnip
Short Play Festival, The Globe Theater, New York, "Audience
Choice Award Winner."

CHARACTERS

NIGEL: effeminate gay man of a certain age (late fifties). Tall with nimble fingers.

MARY: big girl with big bones — thirties/forties. She has enormous feet.

SETTING

N & N Women's Shoes — a rather old and slightly shabby shoe store on a forgotten side street in Manhattan.

TIME

Tonight. 8:56 PM.

•   •   •

Lights up. N&N Women's Shoes, an ancient, rather rundown shoe store on a neglected side street of Manhattan. The shoes displayed are top-notch, but the store's fixtures look like they had their heyday in the early 70s. Nigel, a slightly effeminate man who looks like his heyday was also in the early 70s, can be seen standing behind the cash register, reading a women's fashion magazine — W. He is tall and his hair is receding. He is humming "These Boots Were Made for Walking." He glances at his watch and notices that it's time to close. He then grabs a box of shoes from the floor and exits offstage right. He moves briskly with a bit of bounce in his step.

Mary enters the shop. She is a big girl — big bones, big hair, big breasts, big . . . everything. She is wearing a very fashionable, stylish dress. It looks like hell on her. She walks cautiously, like her feet hurt.

As Mary enters, the lights go out — as though Nigel has turned out the lights from the back room.

MARY: Hello?

(Nigel re-enters. He sees Mary and stops.)

NIGEL: Oh, boy.

MARY: Are you closed?

NIGEL: Uh-huh.

(Mary begins to lose her composure.)

MARY: Oh . . . uh . . . Really?

NIGEL: Uh-huh.

MARY: Yes . . . well . . . I'm . . . Oh . . .

(Mary begins to exit. Her feet are killing her and she's on the verge of tears.)

NIGEL: Wait a minute.

(Mary turns expectantly.)

Is that a Galliano?

MARY: What?

NIGEL: Your dress. Is it a knockoff or did I see Naomi Campbell wear it in Bryant Park last fall?

MARY: My mother picked it out.

NIGEL: Expensive taste.

MARY: If you knew how many fittings I had to endure.

NIGEL: What's a girl like you doing in Dior?

(Mary is thrown by the comment. She begins to cry hysterically.)

NIGEL: What? . . . *(Realizing:)* Oh . . . I guess that wasn't . . . I shouldn't have . . . Oh, boy.

MARY: You're right. I look like a knocked-up sow in a silk party dress . . . Like a whole hog stuffed into in a pink satin sausage.

NIGEL: . . . no . . .

MARY: That's what she my mother said.

NIGEL: Then she's going blind. Because what I see before me is . . .

MARY: What?

NIGEL: A very lovely woman.

MARY: I'll get out of here so you can close.

NIGEL: Wait. Can't go out like that.

(He hands her a tissue. She uses it to dab her eyes.)

Take a load off your . . . *(Regretting his word choice.)* Sit down. Go ahead. I've got nowhere to go. Believe me. That's why I'm open so late. Nowhere to go.

MARY: Thanks,

(She sits.)

Nice shop.

(Nigel looks around and smiles sadly at the irony.)

MARY: Not many open this late. Believe me. I've checked.

NIGEL: Shoe emergency?

(Mary plops her feet up on the ledge in front of her chair. Her feet are enormous. This is the first time Nigel has seen her feet.)

Jesus Christ!

MARY: That's what they all say.

NIGEL: What size are they?

MARY: 12 Double E . . . if I'm not retaining water and I elevate my feet for an hour before I go out . . .

NIGEL: Oh, boy.

MARY: My shoes are so tight they're killing me. This strap . . . It's like a knife.

I swear I'd be bleeding to death, if these damn things didn't completely cut off my circulation.

NIGEL: How did you manage to get them on?

MARY: My mother . . . I don't even know why I call her that. She's not my mother really. She's married to my father. She did this to me.

NIGEL: How?

MARY: A tub of ice for an hour.

NIGEL: Mother of God!

MARY: *There's no way you're going to my Crystal's engagement party wearing those Goddamned Birkenstocks!*

NIGEL: Not with that dress —

MARY: *(Renewed tears:)* Ohhhh . . .

NIGEL: I'm sorry . . . I . . .

MARY: You don't know what it's like. You don't. To be trapped . . . Completely trapped by your body. I want to be pretty. Just like my stepsister. The belle of the ball. Hell, I'm not greedy. I'll settle for just being presentable. Ahhhhhhh!!!!

NIGEL: *(Struggling to take off her shoe:)* The buckles are stuck.

MARY: Inside . . . inside I'm beautiful, and smart, and glamorous. I feel all that. But then I look at myself in the mirror and . . .

NIGEL: When does the party begin?

(Nigel continues to try pull the shoes off.)

MARY: I'm an hour late already. There wasn't any room for me in the limousine. But in the cab on the way to The Four Seasons, they started to throb so desperately I didn't think I could take it. I've been to every store in Midtown. One look at my feet and they all showed me the door. They're killing me.

(Nigel takes out a box cutter from his back pocket in his hand.)

MARY: What are you going to do with that?

NIGEL: We'll have to cut them off.

MARY: She'll kill me!!

(Nigel cuts the straps with the box cutter. He delicately removes her feet from the shoes. At first Mary is relieved . . .)

. . . Oh . . . Oh . . .

NIGEL: You're free.

MARY: My feet . . . the feeling is come back into my . . . *(Screaming:)* Ahhhhhhhhh!!

(He begins to rub her feet.)

NIGEL: Deep breaths . . . Deep breaths . . .

MARY: Ahhhhhhhhhh!

NIGEL: Don't fight it. Accept the pain.

MARY: What have you done? Now what am I going to do? In twenty minutes I have to be standing in a reception line as the fat ugly stepsister of the most beautiful bride in the world.

MARY: *(Beginning to enjoy the foot rub:)* Oh . . . oh . . . oh . . .

NIGEL: What's your name?

MARY: Mary.

NIGEL: I can help you, Mary.

MARY: How? Have you studied the art of Japanese foot binding or something?

NIGEL: *(Irish brogue:)* A little magic.

(Nigel disappears into the storage room.)

MARY: What?

NIGEL: I'll be right back.

(Nigel disappears into the storage room.)

MARY: I'm usually not like this. I'm not. My father's wife . . . I don't fit into her perfect picture of perfection. You know — thirty-five, morbidly obese, unmarried. If she could just see what I'm really like. In court during my final arguments. Or cross-examining a hostile witness. We don't get much of that in property law . . . but I can be damn effective.

(Nigel reappears with boxes of shoes.)

MARY: And that daughter . . . Can you be a size zero? Is that even possible?

NIGEL: The biggest sizes of the most fabulous shoes on Earth.

(He pulls the shoes out of their boxes and presents them to Mary one at a time. It is like a religious experience for him.)

Manolo Blahnik . . . Jimmy Choo . . . Ferragamo . . . Gucci . . . Pucci . . . Givenchy . . . Givenchy . . . GIVENCHY!!

MARY: They're gorgeous! What sizes?

NIGEL: Mostly 10s and 11s . . .

MARY: Won't work.

NIGEL: They're open-toed sandals.

MARY: No.

NIGEL: Come on . . .

MARY: You don't know what I've been through.

NIGEL: Try.

(Nigel struggles to put the sandal on Mary's foot. It doesn't fit. He tries another. It doesn't fit. He tries another.)

MARY: Oh, God . . . oh God . . .

NIGEL: It's not over yet.

(He tries a bunch more . . . to no avail. One pair left. He picks it up reverently.)

The largest Ferragamo in the Western Hemisphere.

(He shoves it on her foot. She cries out. She looks down at her foot. It's hopeless.)

MARY: Like trying to stuff a hippo into a thimble.

NIGEL: It's the largest shoe in the shop.

MARY: What?!

NIGEL: . . . The open toes and strap extenders . . .

MARY: *(Picking up her sliced shoes:)* My shoes!

NIGEL: . . . I thought it would work. But your feet!

MARY: They're ruined! What am I going to do? She'll kill me!

NIGEL: I'm sorry.

MARY: I have nothing. I can't even get home now. What am I going to do?

(She begins to cry again. He sprints into the back room.)

MARY: He'll forgive me, won't he? He's always said he loves me no matter how big I am. And I've been bigger . . . If you can believe that. He still loves me. She hasn't ruined that too has she? Oh, Daddy . . .

(Nigel re-enters, carrying a pile of old, dusty shoe boxes.)

MARY: What are those?

NIGEL: Shoes.

(He blows dust off the top of one of the boxes.)

MARY: They're kind of dusty, aren't they?

NIGEL: They've been in storage for a few years.

MARY: Decades?

(She takes a shoe out of one of the boxes. It's a sequined pump.)

Good lord.

NIGEL: A classic.

MARY: They're huge . . . and used.

NIGEL: Very gently . . . very respectfully.

MARY: Whose are they?

NIGEL: A friend of mine.

MARY: She stores her shoes here?

NIGEL: A very good friend.

MARY: Why doesn't she keep them in her closet?

NIGEL: She left town . . . suddenly . . . about fifteen years ago. And hasn't come back since.

MARY: Is she OK?

NIGEL: A new part of her life. . . afraid to look back. You get to be a certain age and your youth is just a little too hard to keep up.

MARY: It's very nice of you to keep them for her.

NIGEL: It makes me feel close to her.

MARY: That's sweet . . . What's your name?

NIGEL: Nigel.

MARY: That's sweet, Nigel.

NIGEL: Shall we?

MARY: What size?

NIGEL: 14 C.

MARY: She must be very tall.

NIGEL: About my height . . . in flats.

MARY: 14 C?

NIGEL: *(He removes a pair from a box. It's the exact shade as Mary's dress — or they can be made out of clear vinyl.)*

Oh, Mary. My God, we have a perfect match!

MARY: *(Clapping:)* Oh! *(Suddenly concerned:)* But the heel!

NIGEL: What about it?

MARY: I can't. I've never worn a heel over an inch high.

NIGEL: What?!

MARY: I can't.

NIGEL: That's absurd!

(He slides the shoes onto Mary's feet.)

MARY: Ahhhh . . .

NIGEL: Eureka!

(She tries to stand. But is very wobbly.)

NIGEL: Steady now . . .

(She takes a few tentative steps.)

MARY: It's like I'm walking a tightrope.

(She takes a tumble.)

Oh . . . Oh . . .

NIGEL: Are you OK?

MARY: It's impossible!

NIGEL: Nonsense. You just need to practice.

MARY: Practice? I can't even get up.

(Nigel tries to help Mary stand. But she is very heavy.)

I live in constant fear that I'll fall and break my hip or I won't be able to get back up. That's the worst fear . . . I won't be able to get back up . . .

(Nigel summons some reserve of super-human strength and is able to hoist Mary up.)

Thank God . . . thank God. And thank you, Nigel.

(She almost tumbles backward again. Nigel runs behind her and hoists her back onto her feet. Mary is very distraught.)

I can't . . .

NIGEL: I don't want to hear it. You just need to find that woman inside. The woman you were telling me about. That powerful, confident woman who is so strong and brave . . .

MARY: . . . who wears Birkenstocks every day?

NIGEL: A big, beautiful powerful woman who doesn't take shit from anyone . . .

MARY: Right . . .

NIGEL: Shut up and listen to me, Mary.

(This leaves Mary dumbstruck.)

You can hide behind your little property law practice and your bad eating habits and your insecurities and self-pity until you grow old and lonely or die young. Or you can take this opportunity to finally be proud of who you are. Not the woman you see in the mirror with the big hair and bigger ass . . . but the woman you are inside. The powerful, brilliant, creative, audacious, fun-loving woman who takes the world by the balls and gives them a little twist.

MARY: Excuse me?

NIGEL: A woman who doesn't let anyone tell her what to do, what to eat, what to wear. A woman who is sexy and glamorous . . . who's got a lot to give and knows how to give it. Whose appetite for life is as big as her heart. I want to see that woman . . . that big, bold, beautiful woman. High heels? Please! That woman could strap on snowshoes for an audience with the pope and be able to pull it off in high style. Give me that woman, Mary!

MARY: OK . . .

(She takes a few tentative steps.)

NIGEL: Let it go, girl! You got a stick up your ass. Let it all hang out!

(She moves more freely.)

NIGEL: Give it to me. You own this room. Let me see you own it!

(She laughs and begins to strut a little.)

NIGEL: That's it, honey. Make me feel it. Give me that power. Let me feel it. Give it to me!

(She really starts to get into it. She bobbles a little . . .)

NIGEL: Just a speed bump. Nothing to worry about.

(As she struts up and down the store, Mary gradually transforms into a vivacious woman . . .)

NIGEL: Let me see you shake those va va's and wiggle that voom! Yeah, baby! Yeah! My bodacious baby!

MARY: *(Joyfully:)* My feet!

NIGEL: Feel the power? The thrill of three-inch spikes. There's a reason they're called spikes, Mary. Because they're weapons. Like two 45-caliber pistols strapped to each ankle. Power, Mary. Power.

(As she struts across the room in full stride. She's beautiful.)

MARY: I can do it! I can do it!

(She laughs joyfully.)

NIGEL: Piece of cake.

(She looks at her watch.)

MARY: I'm late! What do I owe you?

NIGEL: What? Nothing.

MARY: But the shoes . . .

NIGEL: She'll understand.

MARY: Could you thank her for me? You never told me her name . . .

NIGEL: Nelly. Nelly Forbush.

MARY: That name sounds familiar.

NIGEL: A musical star . . . of sorts.

MARY: Really?

NIGEL: Mostly cabaret. A few select venues down on Greenwich.

MARY: I might have seen her perform.

NIGEL: Doubt it. Long time ago. Different life. Before she got old . . . and tired.

MARY: I hope she's OK.

NIGEL: She's fine. She writes occasionally.

MARY: I have to give you something . . . for the shoes.

NIGEL: Nelly's an old trooper. She'd understand.

MARY: She sounds like an amazing woman.

NIGEL: Nelly? She's a sassy old broad.

MARY: *(She smiles at Nigel with a twinkle in her eye.)*

(Directly to Nigel:) Thank you, Nelly.

(He blushes.)

NIGEL: Come back tomorrow and tell me how it goes.

MARY: *(Suddenly nervous:)* Oh . . .

NIGEL: You can do it. They're magic shoes. They'll get you through this.

MARY: I'm a powerful woman. I'm a powerful woman. I'm a powerful woman . . .

(She repeats the mantra as she exits the shop.)

NIGEL: You go, girl!

(After she leaves, Nigel crosses back into the room. He sees the red-sequined stiletto pumps. He holds them reverently. He removes his shoes and slowly puts them on. He revels in the act of buckling them on. He rises to his feet and poses.)

(He crosses to center stage and turns his back to the audience.)

(He takes off his glasses. The song "I Will Survive" plays. He turns and lip-synchs the lyrics. He has a completely choreographed routine. He's amazing. This goes on for a while.)

Nelly, girl. You still got it!

(He stops in front of the mirror. He squints to see himself in the mirror. He puts his glasses back on. Then he sees his reflection in the mirror and freezes. He slowly loses his posture, his poise, his presence. His shoulders droop and he looks awkward in the heels. He is back to being Nigel. He looks closer. And then he discovers Nigel again. He is surprised to discover that he likes what he sees after all.)

Hello there, Nigel.

(He smiles a beautiful smile.)

(Lights fade.)

END OF PLAY

Youngsters

BRIAN DYKSTRA

Youngsters was commissioned and performed by The Drilling Company with Hamilton Clancy, Artistic Director, in the spring of 2005 at the 78th street Theatre Lab. It was directed by Peter Bretz and featured Karen Kitz and Eirik Gislasson.

CHARACTERS

GORDON: early thirties, a teacher

PAULA: late forties, professorial

SETTING

Paula's office

•   •   •

Paula sits, waiting and working on some paperwork. Gordon enters, as if looking for Paula.

GORDON: There you are.

PAULA: You mean here in my office?

GORDON: Right.

PAULA: OK.

GORDON: I've come to a decision.

PAULA: Hold on a minute.

GORDON: I've decided.

PAULA: I hear you, but it seems quick.

GORDON: I know what I'm doing.

PAULA: I'm sure you do, but I want you to think about it some more.

GORDON: I don't need to.

PAULA: "Fools rush in . . . "

GORDON: Do you somehow know what I've decided?

PAULA: No.

GORDON: Then how do you know I'm rushing in?

PAULA: Are you?

GORDON: . . . Not really the point.

PAULA: You're not going to send it.

GORDON: Yes, I am.

PAULA: No, you're not.

GORDON: Yes, I am.

PAULA: Why?

GORDON: You know why.

PAULA: I want to hear you say it.

GORDON: You already know.

PAULA: No, I only think I know.

GORDON: He can't do what he's doing.

PAULA: But why do you want to send it?

GORDON: It's wrong.

PAULA: Wrong?

GORDON: Yes.

PAULA: OK, but what are you hoping to get out of sending it?

GORDON: I'm hoping to right this wrong.

PAULA: Yes, fine, but is there nothing about this that's between you and Peter, something about evening up some kind of score?

GORDON: What are you suggesting?

PAULA: He's a very popular teacher.

GORDON: I'm not that shallow.

PAULA: She's a very fetching girl.

GORDON: What am I hearing?

PAULA: Is there part of you that feels the need to get even?

GORDON: Let me be clear, nothing about this is about vengeance.

PAULA: Vengeance? See, that's a surprise. The word I would have used was *revenge*.

GORDON: Is there a substantive difference?

PAULA: Not that I'm aware of. Except for the fact the one you chose is traditionally the domain of The Lord.

GORDON: The Lord?

PAULA: That's right.

GORDON: We're talking about The Lord now?

PAULA: In this climate, we'd be fools not to.

GORDON: So, what's your point? Are you making some point with that old, "Vengeance is Mine" is that what you're doing?

PAULA: Yes. "Sayeth The Lord." You have some kind of God complex going on I'm not aware of?

GORDON: So, OK, Revenge, then. "A meal best served cold."

PAULA: A dish.

GORDON: OK, a dish, of course a dish, I know that. "A dish best served cold." I know that. I don't have any idea why I'd say a meal . . . But, wait, you know what? The truth is, it's not about revenge *or* vengeance.

PAULA: It's not?

GORDON: No, it's about justice.

PAULA: That's what you say. But we both know it's not entirely about justice.

GORDON: We do?

PAULA: Sure. Because you just now committed to revenge after not wanting to commit to vengeance. If it was really about justice, you wouldn't feel the need to make the distinction.

GORDON: Stop talking like I'm a student in one of your classes.

PAULA: Forgive me. Occupational hazard. As you well know. But, I've been thinking about it too, about you sending that letter; and what I've arrived at, is you are not sending that letter.

GORDON: You sound pretty sure.

PAULA: Oh, I'm pretty sure.

GORDON: What if I do send it?

PAULA: Then I'm going to show you just how cold revenge can get.

GORDON: Are you threatening me?

PAULA: Am I threatening you?

GORDON: Yeah.

PAULA: You mean when I said, "I'm going to show you how cold revenge can get?"

GORDON: Yeah. Is that some kind of threat?

PAULA: I hate that question. That's like walking in on a family member, balled up in a corner, bleeding from her ears, rocking back and forth, crying so hard, her clothes are wet. You go over, concerned, you lean down, put your hand on her shoulder and ask gently, "Are you OK?" But it's a stupid question, isn't it? Of course she's not OK. Any idiot can see she's not OK. So, let me frame in your question for you, "Am I threatening you?"

GORDON: Of course you are.

PAULA: Of course I am. You know how we could tell? It was when I said, "I'm going to show you how cold revenge can get." See, how could that be anything but a threat? I mean, really now, in what context could that possibly be construed as not a threat?

GORDON: So I guess my question is, *why* are you threatening me?

PAULA: Why do you want to send that letter?

GORDON: It's a fundamental transgression.

PAULA: That's just —

GORDON: It's clearly wrong. It's so clearly wrong, it's punishable by dismissal, and there's good reason for that. Teachers sleeping with students, what is she, twenty? If that?

PAULA: Just a poor little lamb.

GORDON: It is clearly a violation of the trust she is required to put in her teacher.

PAULA: That big bad wolf.

GORDON: He's taken advantage of that trust.

PAULA: Blah, blah, blah.

GORDON: He has!

PAULA: So, what?

GORDON: So what? What do you mean, so what? We're watching a girl, a child, get put through the kind of emotional ringer that not only isn't fair to her, it might really be damaging.

PAULA: And, what, it takes a village to raise this child?

GORDON: Why are you being —

PAULA: And you're the self-appointed sheriff of all that is moral in our little village?

GORDON: Why this cavalier? You know I'm right.

PAULA: Why did you let it go on so long? Sheriff. You knew he was seeing this girl socially. It wasn't like they were being all that discreet. Why did you let it go on?

GORDON: I thought it was none of my business.

PAULA: What changed?

GORDON: She's in love with him.

PAULA: And?

GORDON: You see that, right?

PAULA: I do.

GORDON: So, something needs to be done.

PAULA: Not what you propose.

GORDON: Why not?

PAULA: Because if you send that letter, I'm going to hear about it. And when I hear about it, I'm going to compose a remarkably similar letter. But the subject of my letter will be you. I will accuse you, in my letter of having an affair with a student here. But, unlike you, I will sign my name to it and I will stand by it, after I send a copy to your wife.

GORDON: Why would you do that? It's not even true.

PAULA: Will your wife know it isn't true?

GORDON: Yes.

PAULA: How?

GORDON: . . . OK, so she won't. Why would you do that?

PAULA: Because she won't know it isn't true. How could she? None of our spouses would. That's the position we're in. All of us. That's how precarious our jobs are. We work with these children, and I take offense at that characterization, children, my ass. These kids don't know what they're doing when they crawl into the sack with a teacher? Please.

GORDON: This one's in over her head.

PAULA: And I feel for the girl. I do. It's sad. So she'll work through her daddy complex, get a better grade than she deserves, and chalk it up to her first tragic affair. If she's lucky, it might even make her a better writer. I've read her work, it couldn't hurt.

GORDON: That's really the way you want to say that?

PAULA: What position would you have me take? You want to make this a thing? There are hundreds of students coming through here every year. You really feel that secure you're not going to meet one down the road who pushes all your buttons?

GORDON: Of course not! You mean have an affair with a student? Of course not!

PAULA: If your letter gets sent, and Pete gets dismissed because of it, you will have demonstrated to these children just how much power they possess. Even if he doesn't get dismissed. These students will realize an anonymous letter accusing a teacher of marital infidelity, or of seducing (or being seduced) by a student throws this administration into a tizzy. You think we won't have to deal with a spate of accusations that might touch any one of us?

GORDON: You're having one, too.

PAULA: Don't be ridiculous.

GORDON: But you've had one?

PAULA: Who hasn't?

GORDON: I haven't.

PAULA: You're young yet, give yourself another semester. And so what? It's the pitiful, worst-kept secret of higher education. Hopefully higher education. And, I'm saying we're all at risk. Even you. Even if you're innocent. The rule exists so that if a student wants to bring charges herself, she (or he) has a viable option. But they have to bring it on themselves. The scrutiny, the questions, the innuendo, the public humiliation of having accused, they have to deal with the fallout themselves.

GORDON: So, the victim gets the blame?

PAULA: Victim? No. Other students need to see it's nothing to trifle with. Your letter outs this kid against her will and other students who are in some post teenage competition for the attention of a part-time adjunct, figure out how to get rid of that competition by sending letters accusing all kinds of things. The whole cachet of sexual harassment has finally, mercifully faded a bit. Let's not revisit it. Let's not turn this girl into the first lemming in line.

GORDON: Who are you protecting?

PAULA: You. Obviously. Me. The rest of the faculty. All of us.

GORDON: And this girl?

PAULA: It's a dalliance with a teacher. She's in over her head. Hopefully, she'll drag Peter into some emotional disaster, as well. Hopefully there will be some cost to him for his behavior. Hopefully, when some dark-eyed beauty comes along who reminds you of your first crush, you'll remember how you made room for a fellow teacher a few years back, and hope precedent makes room for you, so some spiteful sculptured prick doesn't put you through the kind of humiliating question & answer — ! . . . And . . . Perhaps, I've said too much. If you do the research, you will find a slight bump in the road of my ivory tower career that lands me at this liberal arts institution at this stage in my life, rather than the slightly more elevated position I had envisioned for myself. And, that being the case, let's be honest, these empty-headed children of leisure who kill brain cells with ecstasy and hip-hop while dressing like whores and desperately search for husbands rather than educations, what's the only thing most of them are good for if not the occasional roll in the hay?

GORDON: Are you serious?

PAULA: How could I be? You want revenge, look for it somewhere else.

GORDON: I don't want revenge.

PAULA: Good. That's safer. Cleaner. Don't want revenge. Look what happens to a person when you do.

GORDON: . . . This is someone different.

PAULA: And your point.

GORDON: . . . What do you have against her?

PAULA: Specifically?

GORDON: Yes.

PAULA: I don't know. I suppose I'm aghast she had the bad taste to choose Peter. As for the rest of them: Now that I'm to live out my days at a second-tier educational institution nowhere near a population center that supports world-class culture or art, not enough of these frat boys want to fuck me, anymore. That's what I have against her. But, not to worry. I'm sure I'll get over it.

(Gordon lingers a moment. Paula gets back to work. Gordon leaves the room. Paula doesn't even look up. She just continues working.)
(Blackout.)

END OF PLAY

Top Floor

DAVID EPSTEIN

Top Floor, by David Epstein, was written expressly for this pub-
lication. The short play has since evolved into a full-length.
Excerpts will be performed at the SEEN Festival, 2008, which
is hosted annually by Invisible City Theater Company.

CHARACTERS
>GARY
>SUSAN

SETTING
>A dimly lit penthouse apartment on the Lower East Side

• • •

Night. A dimly lit penthouse apartment on the Lower East Side. Gary Lane comes through the front door with his wife Susan. In their late thirties, they are a tall, sophisticated couple with smart clothes and tired faces. Susan shakes out a wet umbrella, takes off her coat, and examines the space. Gary sets down his wife's luggage and watches her saunter. It is raining.

GARY: Do you like it?

SUSAN: What have you done?

GARY: You don't like it.

SUSAN: I didn't say that.

GARY: Then what did you say?

SUSAN: Why didn't you tell me?

GARY: I told you.

SUSAN: But you didn't *tell me* tell me. We have an upstairs now?

GARY: Your idea.

SUSAN: Mine?

>*(He takes the umbrella and puts it away.)*

GARY: "We live on the top floor" is what you always used to say. "If we ever make enough we should buy the roof and make this our penthouse suite." Remember?

SUSAN: That was five years ago, Gary.

GARY: *(He nods.)* Uh, huh.

SUSAN: So on a whim you decided to add a floor to our apartment?

GARY: While you were with your parents I had time to think.

SUSAN: Clearly.

>*(He steps up behind her; perhaps runs a finger through her hair.)*

GARY: So much has happened. It was cold this winter. For both of us. Everyone expects so much.

SUSAN: Yes.

GARY: We needed a change so I went ahead and did it.

>*(He kisses the back of her neck. Susan tries to be attentive but is elsewhere.)*

GARY: You don't like it, do you?

SUSAN: I didn't say that. I didn't say anything.

GARY: I *know.*

SUSAN: I like it, Gary. I just walked in. I'm getting used to it. Of course I like it.

GARY: Are you sure?

SUSAN: Of course I'm sure.

GARY: Because you seem undecided.

SUSAN: I'm not undecided. I like it.

(He backs away and admires the room. He then looks to her.)

GARY: *(Long pause.)* Really?

SUSAN: Gary!

GARY: I'm sorry. This is a big deal for me.

SUSAN: I see that. I can only say I like it so many times. It's bigger. Not so cramped. It really is what we always talked about.

GARY: You're not just saying that?

SUSAN: I'm not just saying it.

GARY: So I can show you around?

SUSAN: I wish you would.

GARY: You're not too tired?

SUSAN: *(Warning.) Gary.*

GARY: All right. First let me get your shoes. Don't want to mess up the new floor. Everything is a little out of place but is going to look great in time for spring. The view will blow your mind. There were complaints from the neighbors but that was expected.

SUSAN: About our view?

GARY: About sound, drilling, hammering, portable power generators, cranes in the street, workmen, permits. The place was a disaster zone. But it was worth it. Watch this.

(He pulls on the chord to the blinds. As they open, the lighting brings more color to the room. Susan covers her mouth and giggles.)

SUSAN: You can see the whole city from here. Look at that!

GARY: This will be the living room. The TV goes here. Dining room and kitchen are taking over in the old bedroom. Everything else is on the second floor. Office, weight room, walk in closet, laundry room. The master bedroom is right on top of us. Plus two bedrooms in the back. Right now one of them is . . . Oh! We also get the roof but that won't be ready until summer. There will be a deck and a grill. We can go up and look around when the rain stops. What else?

SUSAN: What about the room?

GARY: What?

SUSAN: You were about to say, "One of the rooms upstairs." What about it?

GARY: Oh. It's nothing. You hungry?

SUSAN: "Nothing"?

GARY: We can still order from Dynasty Bowl. They deliver until two.

SUSAN: I ate on the plane. You're not going to tell me?

GARY: I'm telling you it's not what you think.

SUSAN: Come on, Gary. You asked me to be excited, didn't you?

GARY: Susan —

SUSAN: And now I am excited and want to know even the most insignificant details. You went out on a limb, you made changes to our home, you —

GARY: *(Sharply.)* The bedroom still has the crib in it. There I said it. Let's get depressed now, OK?

(It is some time before he speaks.)

GARY: I've . . . Had a lot of coffee. I was nervous about you seeing the place. I was nervous about seeing you. I still am. I wanted you to like it. I know we can have different tastes. I didn't do all this to try and make you forget.

SUSAN: You just wish I would.

GARY: No, no. That's not what I'm saying.

SUSAN: Then what?

GARY: Once in a while . . . Does it hurt to try?

(Susan wraps herself in her arms. The rain takes over for a moment.)

GARY: Sue?

(No response.)

Have you talked to the museum?

SUSAN: I go back in two weeks.

GARY: I'm sure they miss their curator.

SUSAN: They survived. I don't know if I'm ready. All this time off. You've spoiled me.

GARY: You can take more.

(She gives him a look.)

You don't have to work.

SUSAN: I have to work.

GARY: I mean in the great scheme of our personal economics, we —

SUSAN: I know what you mean. You've told me a thousand times.

GARY: All right —

SUSAN: What did you think? I'd get back in town and still be broken by this thing? Sit here all day and watch you bull and bear over the phone until the bell rings? Cook meals and do macrame?

GARY: Can you stop?

SUSAN: I love my job and I'm going back.

GARY: I'm not arguing.

SUSAN: Things will be different.

GARY: Yes they will.

SUSAN: I'm not looking forward to the questions, that's all. "Where have you been? When can we see the bundle of joy?" Jesus. You've been through it. You know how awful it is to explain. I guess it's different for the man.

GARY: Why do you always say that?

SUSAN: What?

GARY: How do you know it's different? Maybe things are exactly the same. Maybe the idea of us being from different planets is a bunch of garbage we choose to believe in order to keep us from seeing how similar we really are.

SUSAN: That's real deep, sweetheart.

GARY: I'm serious.

SUSAN: I *know*.

GARY: What do you want from me?

(Exhausted.)

Maybe we should get back to trying to forget.

SUSAN: You're right. Let's forget. Novel idea. I think it's high time we forget everything we can as soon as possible.

GARY: I wish you wouldn't do that.

SUSAN: And I wish I could forget as much as you.

GARY: I didn't forget, Susan!

SUSAN: That's right! Because there is no forgetting is there, Gary?! So why bother asking me in the first place?!

(They are horrified with their raised voices. Neither knows what to say. Susan weeps softly.)

SUSAN: I'm sorry. For a lot of things. I'm sorry that I'm crazy.

GARY: You're not crazy. You've been through something.

SUSAN: We're educated people. Raised well. We have friends. I just . . . I can't stop asking myself, you know — Why us?

(Searches the rain.)

GARY: There is no "why." It just is.

SUSAN: Really?

GARY: Yeah.

SUSAN: Interesting. Because when I look back at how our romance began, you always used to say that, "Everything happens for a reason." But when our baby arrives dead to the world, it's, "There is no why"?

(Gives a narrow look.)

There are discrepancies in regard to which events in our life you deem as part of our destiny and which you do not. The way we met? Destiny. Our stillborn baby? Not so much.

GARY: I can't believe you.

SUSAN: What?

GARY: What? It's been six months. You chose to rush off to your parents for a half a year. You had all this time to sit on it. To "adjust." Wasn't that the word and the plan?

SUSAN: But?

GARY: But I don't know, Sue, you tell me. I look at you and I listen and I swear I feel like nothing has changed. I feel like you are still in the same state of shock you were the day you left the hospital. Why did you go away if it wasn't going to help? Why force us to go through this alone, if — You've been home ten minutes and you're picking fights?

SUSAN: You're the one who said there was an empty crib upstairs.

GARY: I did, but that isn't exactly how I described it, is it?

SUSAN: What difference does it make how you describe it?

GARY: It makes a big difference! I didn't want to talk about it.

SUSAN: Well, the next time you don't want to talk about something maybe you shouldn't bring it up.

GARY: Jesus. I can't believe we're doing this.

SUSAN: Believe it.

GARY: You've barely scratched the surface of this thing, have you?

(For a moment they are looking at each other. He breaks off. The rain seems to keep them cooled.)

SUSAN: Tell me something.

GARY: What more do you want me to say? Everything gets me in trouble.

SUSAN: I, for one, am tired of hearing myself speak. Aren't you?

(Faint smile.)

Besides. You're better at the truth.

GARY: There is a ton of mail. Everyone sent letters of congratulations.

(He sets a small stack of cards on the table. He watches her sift through before revealing another stack.)

GARY: Two weeks later, most of the same people sent condolences.

SUSAN: How weird.

GARY: Twilight Zone.

(They sit quietly, staring at the two piles.)

GARY: You think we can we get through this?

SUSAN: It's not that much mail.

GARY: That's not what I mean.

SUSAN: I know.

GARY: We spent six months apart. We prepared ourselves. We talked about not arguing or blaming each other. We said we'd work together to stay happy.

SUSAN: How we doing?

GARY: I'm asking you.

SUSAN: I don't know, Gar. The idea of working to stay happy seems a bit counterproductive. We're either going to be happy or we're not.

GARY: Well? Are we?

SUSAN: I don't know.

(Silence.)

GARY: Do you still love me?

(She does not answer. Gary nods with uncertainty, then goes through the stack. Susan watches for a long beat before she starts to help. The rain begins to fall in sheets. Thunder rumbles. Fade to black.)

END OF PLAY

Lucky

Laura Jacqmin

Lucky was the first place winner in the Ten-Minute Play Competition at the Kennedy Center American College Theater Festival for Region III. It was produced on January 14, 2006, and was directed by Kendra Stock and stage managed by Michelle Engleman. The cast included: Thomas — Christian Duhamel; Zoe — Melissa Law.

CHARACTERS
ZOE
THOMAS

SETTING
The woods

•   •   •

Zoe, fifteen, waits on a bench, a six-pack on the ground by her feet. Thomas, twenties, enters in a heavy-duty rain jacket.

ZOE: Hi.
THOMAS: Hi.
ZOE: I brought beer.
THOMAS: You can't drink.
ZOE: It's for you.
    And I can too drink.
THOMAS: Not legally.
ZOE: There's a lot of stuff I can't do legally.
    Doesn't stop me from doing it.
THOMAS: Maybe I'll have just one.
    (Thomas reaches for the six-pack.)
ZOE: All that's on your mind —
    I figured you would want to be drunk, for this.
    (Thomas decides against a beer.)
THOMAS: There are more trees than I remembered from last year.
ZOE: Did you have a hard time finding me?
THOMAS: No.
ZOE: I mean, we haven't been here in ages.
    The path can be dark.
    I would understand if you had a hard time finding me.
THOMAS: I could see you from the road. In my headlights.
    You looked small.
ZOE: You saw me waiting for you?
    This whole time?
    What was I doing?
THOMAS: I like that shirt.
    (Beat.)

ZOE: You were watching me?

THOMAS: Yes.

> *(Beat.)*

ZOE: The shirt's old; you've seen it before.

> It's my lucky shirt.

THOMAS: I don't remember.

ZOE: I knew you wouldn't.

> I was wearing it the first time you kissed me, a year ago.

THOMAS: Listen! I just came to tell you — that this isn't happening.

> I know what we said earlier, but I just can't. I wanted to tell you, in person.
>
> I owe you that.

ZOE: You do.

THOMAS: — but it's not going to happen. Between us.

> There are a billion reasons why. I'm sure you know them all.
>
> You smell good.

ZOE: I'm wearing perfume. Or *parfoom,* as they call it in Europe.

THOMAS: It's nice. Did you buy it for me?

ZOE: *(She did:)* I did not.

THOMAS: You shouldn't have gone to the trouble.

ZOE: Guess not.

> *(Beat. In retaliation for the slight:)*
>
> How's your brother? By the way.
>
> *(Thomas breaks away toward the exit.)*

THOMAS: I'm out of here.

ZOE: Great. Get gone. See if I care.

> *(Thomas looks back at Zoe.)*

THOMAS: Can I just — kiss you once? Before I go?

ZOE: I guess so.

> *(Zoe smoothes her hair behind her ears, preparing. Beat.)*
>
> Well?

THOMAS: Never mind.

ZOE: You don't have the guts.

THOMAS: I have the guts.

> *(Thomas kisses Zoe. It is a good kiss. They separate awkwardly.)*

ZOE: Do I kiss better than last year?

THOMAS: Yes.

> No.
>
> I don't remember.

ZOE: You've kissed a lot of girls since then, huh?

THOMAS: They all blur together.

Does that hurt your feelings?

ZOE: *(It does:)* No.

THOMAS: Besides, there's nothing special about this — we've already kissed.

This is just a rehash.

ZOE: "A sure thing."

(Silence.)

That's what you told Jim, isn't it? About me?

THOMAS: You're mistaken.

Which Jim? Yoga Jim or Tennis Jim?

ZOE: *(Continued.)* Doesn't matter. I overhear everything you say to people here.

I know the reason you came back.

I know you need money.

I know your brother's —

THOMAS: Don't talk about my brother.

(Beat.)

You're different. You used to be — I don't know — *quieter.*

More . . .

Do you still come here? With other people?

ZOE: Yes.

THOMAS: A lot?

ZOE: A lot of times, or with a lot of guys?

THOMAS: Either.

ZOE: Both.

A lot.

THOMAS: Anybody I know?

ZOE: Probably.

With my boyfriend.

THOMAS: Your *boyfriend.*

ZOE: Yes. My boyfriend.

He's in B-group.

He's extremely mature for his age.

THOMAS: So you brought him out here to . . . ?

ZOE: We just kissed.

We've only come here once. He's from the city. He doesn't like the trees.

THOMAS: His loss.

You know, I thought about this place, that we were going to be in the trees, in the woods. It always used to be so cold.

So I brought my jacket.

ZOE: But it's June. You're sweating.

THOMAS: I couldn't afford the kind that "breathes."

I just — figured we could lie on it.

(To recover:)

So we wouldn't have to lie on the ground.

(Thomas throws the jacket on the ground, between them. They both look at it like it's a dead thing.)

ZOE: We might stain it.

THOMAS: I would take care of that.

I mean — if I was the one who made the stain. Then I'd take care of it.

ZOE: I might bleed.

(Thomas breaks away, grabbing his jacket.)

THOMAS: We should head back so you don't get in trouble.

ZOE: Am I not being sexy enough? Do you need to — get yourself in the mood? I mean, I could say things.

I thought the idea of fucking me was pretty sexy by itself.

THOMAS: Jesus.

Maybe I should have a beer.

ZOE: If you want.

THOMAS: You're probably trying to get me *drunk.*

ZOE: Probably.

(Thomas chugs an entire beer. Zoe watches him.)

Now you're too drunk to drive.

THOMAS: One beer isn't enough to make me stay. When you've been drinking for as long as I have, you build up a tolerance.

ZOE: "As long as I have." Yeah. 'Cause you're such an *old man.* Give it a rest, already.

How many beers *would* make you stay?

THOMAS: There aren't enough in the world.

(Beat.)

ZOE: I haven't washed this shirt since that night you kissed me. I've slept with it under my pillow every single night, for a year. I put it on today and I knew you'd be back, I just knew it.

THOMAS: And here I am.

ZOE: I promise I'm ready for you this time. I wasn't before, but I am now.

I was immature before, but now I'm a capable grown-up. Not some stupid kid.

No matter what you say to Jim about me.

THOMAS: I never told him you were stupid.

ZOE: Don't lie.

I'll like you no matter what you say about me. No matter what the other girls in my group say about *you*.

(*Thomas freezes.*)

THOMAS: You didn't tell anybody you were coming here, did you?

ZOE: What if I did?

(*Beat.*)

Don't be so jumpy.

Can I have a beer?

THOMAS: You're asking my permission?

Yeah, have a beer.

(*Zoe opens a beer and hands it to Thomas. She opens another beer and they both drink.*)

ZOE: See? I'm drinking beer, just like you. Like we're equals.

Just pretend like we're two consenting adults.

THOMAS: OK.

ZOE: Tell me I'm sexy.

THOMAS: You're really sexy.

But that doesn't matter.

(*A test:*)

ZOE: Tell me what you want to do to me.

THOMAS: I want . . .

I want to get lucky.

ZOE: It's kind of a guarantee.

THOMAS: (*Taking over, telling the story:*) Shut up.

I wanna throw you down on the ground, in the mud. Without the coat.

I want to make love to you.

ZOE: Make *love* to me.

Because you love me?

THOMAS: Shut *up.*

And after, I want to drive you back to the grounds and watch you sneak into your cabin.

Through the window. The bathroom window.

And wake everybody up so they'll ask you where you've been — but they'll already know.

They'll know what you did.

ZOE: But they won't know who I did it with.

(*Beat.*)

I won't tell them.

THOMAS: You promise?

ZOE: I promise.

THOMAS: *(Continued.)* Because people who are in positions of power — like me — have to watch out for themselves.

When I see you tomorrow, I'm going to make you swim the whole lake just like all the other kids — no special treatment. Nobody will be able to tell anything.

You *want* this.

I'm not forcing this on you. I'm not abusing my rank.

And after all — there'll be no proof.

You know that, right?

No matter what you tell anybody, I'll deny it.

ZOE: I know.

And *you* know —

That if you *don't* — right now — then I'll go right back and I *will* tell everybody and they'll fire you so fast that they won't even give you the check for your first day and your dad will be so disappointed and the hospital will kick your brother to the curb and it'll be all your fault. *(Silence.)*

So we have a deal.

You're not about to fuck me — we're going to fuck each *other*.

THOMAS: You're different.

You worked some weird shirt voodoo.

ZOE: It brings me luck.

So come on.

You won't regret this.

(Beat.)

THOMAS: Let's go further back in the woods.

I don't want anyone to see.

(Thomas exits. After checking the woods, Zoe follows him.)

END OF PLAY

What I Learned From Grizzly Bears

JESSICA LIND

What I Learned From Grizzly Bears by Jessica Lind was originally produced as part of the Strawberry One-Act Festival at the Riant Theatre in the summer of 2006. It was directed by Amanda Hinkle. The cast: Bernadette — Jessica Lind; Husband — Jason Thomas

CHARACTERS

BERNADETTE: mid-twenties. A biologist with an intense passion for grizzly bears. She is feisty, easily excitable, and a little quirky. She is almost completely oblivious to anything happening around her.

HUSBAND: late twenties. He genuinely loves Bernadette.

TIME

A muddled present

SETTING

The only necessary set piece is a grocery-checking contraption that doubles as a table. Otherwise the actors are on a bare stage.

A NOTE ABOUT THE PLAY

Be aware that the events in this play do not occur in real time. With that in mind, please steer clear of overly literal interpretations.

•   •   •

Bernadette stands behind a table, engrossed in a map of Alaska. She speaks to the audience. A faint beeping noise can be heard.

BERNADETTE: It's not so much for the glory of it. Although, don't get me wrong, who doesn't like a little glory now and then? But I don't want it if it's going to get me sidetracked. All I want is to get out there, be one with the animals. Like Jane Goddall. I mean, she wasn't just a photographer or a researcher . . . she *was* a chimp. And that's what you have to do, you have to *be a chimp.* I'm not so much interested in chimps. Although I haven't completely ruled them out. I'd much rather study predators. Carnivores. I like a little danger. Like if you get too close your face could get ripped off. Who needs a face when you're living with animals? It'd probably be better if you didn't have one. Think if you had no face . . . what a relief. You wouldn't have to get up every morning and moisturize with SPF or pluck or anything. It'd just be you, your arms and legs, your torso and probably your neck. Anyway, the point is that it wouldn't bother me. If that's what it costs to be in there with the carnivores . . . I'll do it.

(Husband enters with groceries. She starts checking them. The beeping gets louder and louder. She's now talking to him.)

I'm thinking grizzlies. OK so it's not a carnivore it's an omnivore. I'm flexible. I just love the way they loom. Big ferocious looming omnivores. Oh good. Kiwi fruit. My favorite. Anyway, I'm mostly interested in studying how a grizzly's diet relates to its behavior. You wouldn't believe how much impact changes in the environment have on a grizzly. The salmon population in Alaska, for example, has been dwindling because of dams and runoff in the rivers which is a huge portion of a grizzly's diet in the summer. And if the salmon are gone, the grizzlies get desperate and when they get desperate they get mean and when they get mean . . . Well, you just better watch out that's what. I'm planning on moving to Alaska to study them. I've already mapped out my research strategy, invested in equipment. All I have to do really is buy my ticket. I mean, there are people out there just dying to give me money. You wouldn't believe how easy it is to get a research grant. This is America buddy you better believe it. Is this parsley?

HUSBAND: Cilantro.

BERNADETTE: I bet you wouldn't believe I was valedictorian of my university, would you? I was. Summa cum laude with a double major and thirty extra credits. Then it was on to graduate school. I'm telling you I am getting pumped. I'm finally finished with school and I am blazing. Nothing is stopping me from getting on a plane tomorrow. I'm on my way up! I'm standing on the edge of the diving board, ready to jump and all I have to do is —

HUSBAND: Don't stand on that.

BERNADETTE: What?

HUSBAND: You can't stand on that.

BERNADETTE: Oh, right. Sorry.

(She lies down on what is now a table. She's completely oblivious to what's going on around her. The beeping noise is faster now, and more muffled sounding. Husband is feeling her stomach.)

There's something fascinating about communicating with animals in their own language. I'm really looking forward to discovering how grizzlies communicate. Oh I've read all the books and all that, but I'm talking about specifics. How does a grizzly sound when she's sad? What do the different pitches and rhythms in their growls mean? What noises do they make when making love? *(Sitting up.)* I'd imagine it's a kind of "uhh uhhh" kind of grunting. You know like —

HUSBAND: Please lie down.

BERNADETTE: Geez you're bossy. Anyway, these are the things I'm looking forward to.

(The beeping is so loud now she's shouting over it.)

I've been applying for all kinds of grants. I have a pretty good chance at getting a research grant through my university. Hey, could you turn that thing down? I can't even hear myself talk. Geez. My research advisor is actually on the board so my chances of getting the grant are really high.

HUSBAND: Congratulations.

BERNADETTE: Well, thanks, but I haven't exactly gotten it yet. But thank you. You're a real sweetie. What did you say your name was?

HUSBAND: It's twins.

BERNADETTE: Twins? What kind of a name is that?

(Mounds of baby stuff, i.e., diapers, stuffed animals, strollers, etc . . . pile up on top of her. She is being buried. She continues talking through it all, oblivious to what's happening.)

Anyway, they only give it to alumni and I'm really the only one qualified. Well, there's this one other guy but he's all into beetles and I'm sure if it came down to choosing between beetles and grizzlies, they'd choose grizzlies. I'd feel like a real loser if I chose beetles over grizzlies. No offense to beetles or anything, but really when it comes down to it I'm sure they'd much rather be associated with grizzlies. As opposed to beetles. *(Realizing she's buried.)* Wow, it's getting stuffy in here. Is anyone else stuffy? Um, "Twins," is it? You wanna help me out of here? I have no idea how all this stuff got here. Pretty inconvenient though I must say. Hey! I'm buried alive here. A little help please . . .

HUSBAND: Don't worry, I'll help you.

BERNADETTE: Great.

HUSBAND: That's what I'm here for, right?

BERNADETTE: I don't know. Is it?

HUSBAND: For better or worse.

(He unburies her.)

BERNADETTE: Wow. You're a real nice guy. A real good-looker too. *(Seeing his finger.)* Crap, you're married. Figures. Oh well. Do you have a brother?

HUSBAND: No. It's just me.

BERNADETTE: Just my luck. Well? . . .

HUSBAND: Well what?

BERNADETTE: Who are you?

HUSBAND: I'm your husband.

BERNADETTE: What are you talking about?

HUSBAND: We're married.

BERNADETTE: That's not possible.

HUSBAND: Check your finger.

(She does. She's wearing a ring.)

BERNADETTE: Well Happy Birthday, this is news to me.

HUSBAND: Your birthday is in October.

BERNADETTE: How do you know?

HUSBAND: I'm your husband.

BERNADETTE: What else do you know?

HUSBAND: You wear a size eight shoe you wash your hair at night and you hate those little marshmallows that come with instant hot chocolate.

BERNADETTE: What do you do?

HUSBAND: I'm an insurance agent.

BERNADETTE: *(Singing.)* "Like a good neighbor, State Farm is there."

HUSBAND: I'm with AllState.

BERNADETTE: Super. Do you cook?

HUSBAND: No. You do that.

BERNADETTE: Do you clean?

HUSBAND: You do that too.

BERNADETTE: What do you do around here then? Water the plants?

HUSBAND: I usually sit in that brown recliner and flip channels until I fall asleep. Then you wake me up when it's time for bed.

BERNADETTE: Wow. It looks like I've won the husband lottery. You can sleep in that chair for all I care.

HUSBAND: Fine.

BERNADETTE: Fine.

HUSBAND: Fine.

BERNADETTE: Fine. *(Pause.)* Was that our first fight?

HUSBAND: No. We have them all the time.

BERNADETTE: What do we fight about?

HUSBAND: Cooking and cleaning.

BERNADETTE: Well, maybe if you'd do it once in a while we wouldn't fight about it. *(Pause.)* Did I make it to Alaska?

HUSBAND: No.

BERNADETTE: Why not?

HUSBAND: You fell in love with me.

BERNADETTE: Why did I do that?

HUSBAND: You thought I looked like Tom Cruise.

BERNADETTE: Do you?

HUSBAND: Nope.

BERNADETTE: Well that was dumb. Where do we live?

HUSBAND: At the end of a cul-de-sac. In a beige house with a beige garage.

BERNADETTE: Why so much beige?

HUSBAND: Development regulations.

BERNADETTE: I feel dizzy.

HUSBAND: You just had twins.

BERNADETTE: Is that what that was? Huh. I didn't see that one coming.

HUSBAND: You did beautifully. You are beautiful.

BERNADETTE: What are you, trying to get me in the sack again? Geez.

HUSBAND: We have to wait six weeks.

BERNADETTE: Lucky me.

HUSBAND: You have to heal first. There was some tearing of the vaginal —

BERNADETTE: Yuck! Alright? Seriously. No need to elaborate.

HUSBAND: *(Pulling out some gum.)* Gum?

BERNADETTE: How can you think of gum at a time like this?

HUSBAND: I don't know. I just thought —

BERNADETTE: You know what? You can take your gum and your recliner and your babies and just shove them. Alright? This is nuts. You make me sick.

HUSBAND: *(Pulling out some Tums.)* Tums?

BERNADETTE: What are you, a Duane Reade or something? What the hell else do you have in there?

HUSBAND: *(Emptying his pockets.)* A toothpick, thirty-two cents, a movie stub from *Must Love Dogs* —

BERNADETTE: Ugh. Don't you ever wash your pants?

HUSBAND: *(Continuing.)* My inhaler, a pacifier, three tropical-flavored Starbursts, and a picture of you and the babies.

(He eats a Starburst.)

BERNADETTE: Let me see that. *(Looking at picture.)* Is this them?

HUSBAND: Uh huh.

BERNADETTE: A boy and a girl?

HUSBAND: *(Beaming.)* Yeah.

BERNADETTE: They're cute.

HUSBAND: They have your eyes.

BERNADETTE: And your weird chin.

(He offers her a Starburst.)

BERNADETTE: No thanks. I hate yellow ones.

HUSBAND: What about red?

BERNADETTE: I'll take a red.

(Their hands touch.)

HUSBAND: I've missed you.

BERNADETTE: Don't get all sappy on me just because we're sharing a Starburst.

HUSBAND: Will you come home with me?

BERNADETTE: That's crazy. I don't want to think about it.

HUSBAND: Where will you go?

BERNADETTE: Alaska. I'm going to go study the grizzlies. You wouldn't believe what it's like to see one of them up close. I mean, I've never actually seen one up close, except for in a zoo, but I don't really count that because their personalities have been altered by human intervention. Anyway, I'm going to Alaska to study them. I'll be living in a tent for the summer when the bears are in the peak of their activity. Then when they go into hibernation, I'll be compiling all my data.

HUSBAND: What should I do with the babies?

BERNADETTE: I don't know. Give them to someone who wants them. Maybe someone who can't have babies.

HUSBAND: But I love them. I can't just give them away.

BERNADETTE: Well, maybe you should have thought about it before you knocked me up.

HUSBAND: You wanted them.

BERNADETTE: What? That's impossible. Why would I all of a sudden want a litter of babies? That's ridiculous. Ludicrous! Don't you know me at all? Didn't you just hear what I said? I'm going to Alaska! People don't live in tents with babies while closely observing grizzly bears. It's just not safe.

HUSBAND: I'll go with you. We'll live in an RV.

BERNADETTE: Yeah. Maybe we can live in a van and park it down by the river. No. Absolutely not. You're not in the picture, do you understand? Nowhere in this picture, which I am standing in, alone, by myself, is there room for you and your weird chin and all those babies.

HUSBAND: This comes as quite a shock.

BERNADETTE: Yeah, well . . . if you have a heart attack over it at least you're with AllState.

HUSBAND: Won't you miss them?

BERNADETTE: I never wanted them.

HUSBAND: That's not true. You said you were ready for a change. You wanted to make a family. You were excited to start a new life.

BERNADETTE: I said all that?

HUSBAND: You did. And you also said you loved me. You said "Life is perfect with you in it." You said that.

BERNADETTE: Maybe I was doped up on NyQuil.

HUSBAND: You meant it when you said it. Anyway, I don't want you to come home with me if you feel this way. I don't want to invade your personal picture or self-portrait or whatever you call it. Good luck. Good luck with your bears.

(He kisses her on the cheek. She kisses him back. It becomes something compelling.)

BERNADETTE: You do kinda look like Tom Cruise.

HUSBAND: It's the chin.

BERNADETTE: So long.

HUSBAND: It's not really so much long as —

BERNADETTE: No, I meant, "So long" as in good-bye.

HUSBAND: Oh. OK. Good-bye Bernadette. I'll miss you.

BERNADETTE: Good-bye.

(He exits. Bernadette addresses the audience.)

You really have to be careful because mother grizzlies will fight to the death for their cubs, ripping the flesh of any animal, no matter how large, if her cubs are threatened. If prematurely separated, her cubs have little to no chance of survival. They usually die either of starvation or in the jaws of a predator. If they do survive, chances are their ability to properly socialize has been severely disrupted. The mother will often wander aimlessly for days, sometimes even weeks, in search of her lost cubs. She shows outward signs of depression, her shoulders droop, her walk slows, she no longer looms but kind of shuffles along — wandering aimlessly along. She loses her majestic dignity, her confidence, and sometimes even her will to eat. The bond between a mother bear and her cubs is extraordinary. The affection and gentleness she displays with them is one of nature's gorgeous mysteries.

(She looks to where he exited. Lights.)

END OF PLAY

9 Hours to Fallujah

CRAIG MCNULTY

Dedicated to Austin Pendleton

9 Hours to Fallujah was originally performed as a semi-finalist in the 12th Annual New York City 15-minute play festival presented by the Turnip Theatre Company in association with the American Globe Theatre in April 2006. It was directed by Craig McNulty. The cast was as follows: Sophia Remolde as Maureen (aka "Mo") Jackson; Matthew Tischler as Brian Alyesworth.

CHARACTERS

MAUREEN JACKSON (aka "Mo"): twenty-two, marine reservist. She wants to be a teacher. She was part of a convoy that was attacked by insurgents, where she fought bravely and remained very calm and very cool — what Hemingway would've called *grace under fire.*

BRIAN ALYESWORTH: twenty-one, Marine reservist. Engineering major and film fanatic, but the type of guy who would be more into *Scarface* than *Breathless.*

TIME

November 8, 2004, 9:30 PM

SETTING

Iraq, U.S.A. military camp just outside of Fallujah

NOTE

(/) denotes actors coming in hard on last word or interrupting.

•   •   •

AT RISE: Sounds of explosions to a black stage. Lights come up on Brian (twenty-one) seated on an army blanket and writing in a journal. He has his shoes off and has articles spread around the blanket (towels, shirts, food rations). Coming up behind him is Maureen (a.k.a. "Mo") (twenty-two) holding a handgun. Brian is consumed with writing in his journal and doesn't see her. She is looking intensely at him. She puts the gun away, takes a swig off a flask, and begins to sneak up on him. Even as she is standing right behind him and reading over his shoulder Brian still doesn't know she's there. She grabs him under his arm and says —

MO: Private Alyesworth.
    (Brian jumps, sending his book flying.)
BRIAN: Jesus Christ Mo! You scared the living shit outta me.
MO: See, if I was a suicide bomber, you'd be dead.
BRIAN: If you were a suicide bomber we'd both be dead.
MO: Yea, but, you be burning in the infidel fires of hell and I'd be in Allah's paradise.
BRIAN: With the rivers of honey and the seventy-two virgins?
MO: Yep. But I don't get how that's supposed to be an incentive, I mean, I'm not gay or even an occasional switch-hitter, so the seventy-two hottie Arab

chicks don't do it for me. And seventy-two male virgins, what would that be, seventy-two teenage Arab boys who's idea of foreplay is throwing me to the ground for a session of amour that lasts all of sixty-four seconds? Wow, whoopee, that's a helluva a paradise for a girl to look forward to.

BRIAN: Maybe the men would look like Omar Sharif or Valentino.

MO: *(Considers this.)* Yea . . . Nah, that still doesn't do it for me.
(Interrupted by three particularly loud explosions in the distance.)
I don't think the locals will be too happy to see the Stars and Stripes tomorrow.

BRIAN: Softening the enemy is the going expression . . . Yea, probably as effective as kicking a junkyard dog in the balls a couple of times thinking it's going to make him more docile.

MO: I understand El General gave a riveting speech yesterday

BRIAN: Invoking the usual suspects: sands of Iwo Jima, shores of Tripoli, John Wayne, John Rambo.

MO: He's seen *Patton* a few too many times.

BRIAN: El general was a "hero" in the epic war against Grenada.
Two years ago smoking a bowl and watching *Full Metal Jacket* never thought my ass would be in this position.

MO: None of us did Bri . . . Just pay close attention to the children.

BRIAN: What?

MO: When the main fighting is going on they'll be gone. When things calm down and you'll see kids around, then the area is probably clear. Not absolutely but probably . . . but if the kids are around, then they all suddenly seem to split, that's when you know the shit is definitely hitting the fan.

BRIAN: OK.

MO: The first time you see someone shooting at you, I mean you can see their face, you're going to be tempted to go for a head shot, don't. Just remember like it was back in basic and aim for the torso . . .
(Mo's now looking through Brian's CD case.)
Jesus, Limp Bisket isn't really your favorite band, is it?

BRIAN: What? Oh, not really. Jerry gave it to me, said it was good rolling out music.

MO: I would just hate to think of anyone dying and the last thing they listened to is Limp Bisket.
(Mo throws CD upstage.)

BRIAN: Mo!

MO: Or Eminem, he's such an asshole.
(Mo throws Eminem CD as well.)

BRIAN: Mo, will you stop fucking with my shit!

MO: OK, just trying to help.

BRIAN: Just don't touch my stuff.

MO: If you had one thing to listen to before you checked out what would it be?

BRIAN: I don't know. Maybe something by U2 or maybe Nirvana . . . tough question.

MO: It is a tough question. When I'm feeling down I listen to Bob Marley and I feel better, or I listen to Bright Eyes and it makes me feel worse . . . but in a good way.

BRIAN: Who the fuck is Bright Eyes?

MO: It's the music I played that night, don't you remember?

BRIAN: Yea, I remember.

(Mo takes letter out of her pocket.)

MO: So I found this under my pillow . . .

BRIAN: Yea, well, you weren't supposed to read it till Thursday. See where it says on the outside, Do not read till Thursday?

MO: Well you didn't date it genius, so for all I knew you meant last Thursday which would've made it a OK for me to read it today.

BRIAN: Oh, is that it? Guess I should've been more specific.

MO: Guess so, and who do you know that would get a letter that says don't open till Thursday and would actually wait for Thursday?

BRIAN: I had this nightmare. I had it more than once. There's all these soldiers who've had their arms, legs, and faces blown off, and they're burned . . . badly. I'm nervous to see them. I'm afraid to be in the same room with them because I'm afraid I'll lose my shit and come off looking like a wuss. So all these dismembered soldiers are dressed up in various outfits, like Hawaiian shirts and football jerseys told how good they look and wheeled around to try to make them feel better, and the whole thing is horrific . . .

MO: It's like so OK to be scared the night before, you wouldn't be human if you/

BRIAN: /Been really sensitive last few days to sensations in my fingers and toes

MO: Is there something wrong with/

BRIAN: /There's nothing wrong, I've just been thinking I don't wanna go home like Stevens or Washington . . .

MO: Or like that guy in *The Sun Also Rises* who gets his balls blown off.

BRIAN: Who was in that?

MO: I don't know, it wasn't a movie.

BRIAN: I think it was.

MO: Jesus, did you ever have to take a liberal arts class or have a summer reading list?

BRIAN: Yea, but that's why God invented Cliff Notes, right?

MO: Whatever . . . in the book by Hemingway the protagonist gets his balls blown off in World War One, or maybe it was his penis? Either way his equipment isn't up for the job anymore . . .

BRIAN: Thanks Mo, that's a helluva story to tell someone the night before/ a major operation.

MO: /Sorry sorry sorry, I know, bad Mo, mouth going before I was thinking.

BRIAN: Yea, well, anything like that and I want you to/

MO: /Now, getting shot in the leg, the fleshy part, not hitting bone, if you had to get it that would be the best place to get shot, with as low a caliber as possible. You'd get a Purple Heart and a one-way trip to Germany with that one.

BRIAN: Listen Mo, I'm Catholic . . .

MO: OK, and I'm a Methodist, what does that/ got to do with anything

BRIAN: /If my legs or arms or dick or face were blown off I'd just as quick stick my gun in my mouth and blow my brains to Syria . . . but being a motherfucking Roman Catholic ya can't kill yourself . . . I guess you can kill as many other cats as you want and still see heaven . . . just not yourself

MO: Never thought of you as being very religious.

BRIAN: Mo, a hot shot of as much morphine as you can get a hold of and just let me go off to sleep.

MO: *(Furious.)* How the fuck can you ask me to do something like that?!

BRIAN: I just thought that we, I'm asking you because/

MO: /It wasn't the booze.

BRIAN: The?/

MO: /I just wanted you to know/

BRIAN: /That?/

MO: /I wasn't with you for an evening's entertainment or . . . it wasn't like that for me.

BRIAN: Yea, well, me too. For an evening's "entertainment" I usually play poker or something, but not that.

MO: I don't want you to think because I'm saying no to this that I don't/

BRIAN: /OK OK OK, it's fine, really.

MO: Can we just talk, like talk talk for a few minutes?

BRIAN: What difference would it make?

MO: Because if we were at school together and you were getting into a bus and riding out of town for summer break it wouldn't be a big deal, right? Sure, I might get killed in a car accident or OD on meth, but chances are none of that would happen. Chances are whatever we'd wanna work out between us/

BRIAN: /So it was a big favor to ask of you and you don't feel too swell about doing it, fine. I don't know if I could look into your eyes and do it for you, but right now there's nothing else to talk about.

MO: Brian, it's just more complicated than how I feel about you/

BRIAN: /you wanna tell me, what? That you're not a slut, that you don't sleep around? Great, thank you. I never thought you were. A few hours from now that information is going to be useful to me . . . how?

MO: Yea . . . no . . . I don't know . . .

(Brian goes back to futzing around with his backpack, Mo gets up and begins to leave.)

We'll always have Iraq . . . during the winter time . . . in the middle of the Jihad . . . right?

BRIAN: Right . . .

(Brian stops futzing with his bag, stands up.)

You know I've never seen *Casablanca*.

MO: Really?

BRIAN: Nope, just never got around to it.

(Mo takes a long look at Brian.)

MO: You will. Trust me.

BRIAN: Maybe.

MO: Did you mean what you wrote at the bottom of the letter?

BRIAN: Yea, but I think you knew that already.

(Mo slowly walks over to Brian, she runs her hand over his face and they share an intense kiss.)

MO: I love you, too, asshole.

(Mo exits quickly stage right.)

BRIAN: Maureen, wait! Shit!

(Brian goes to grab his boots to chase her when he is shot in the leg, in the calf.)

AHH!!!

(Three sharp whistle blasts from stage right.)

MO: *(Offstage.)* Sniper Action Northwest Corner, incoming!

(Prolonged machine-gun blasts offstage, Mo enters stage right with her weapon drawn and kneels next to wounded Brian.)

BRIAN: MO! What the fuck did you do?!/

(Mo grabs a towel and begins to wrap Brian's leg.)

MO: /I got you covered baby, don't worry, I got you covered.

(Lights to black as machine-gun bursts continue.)

END OF PLAY

Black Paintings

NEIL OLSON

Black Paintings by Neil Olson was originally commissioned and produced for Revenge, by The Drilling Company (artistic director Hamilton Clancy). It was presented at 78th Street Theatre Lab in New York City, June 3–19, 2005. Stage Manager/Billie Davis, Scenic Design/Paul Gelinas, Lighting Design/Dans Sheehan, original live music by Tom Garvey, Director/Bradford Olson. Cast: Eric — Hamilton Clancy; Diane — Brigitte Barnett.

CHARACTERS

ERIC

DIANE

SETTING

A room in a house

•   •   •

Diane sits center stage at a table upon which there is a small cardboard box. Eric stands stage right at a set of open French doors, looking out.

ERIC: Can you see the ocean from here?

DIANE: Yes.

ERIC: Where do I look?

DIANE: South.

ERIC: Which way is that?

DIANE: The way you're facing.

ERIC: I'm not seeing it.

DIANE: That's right. *(He turns and looks at her in confusion.)* You asked if *I* could see the ocean. There are lovely views from the bedrooms upstairs, but since you will never see those bedrooms, you will never see the ocean from here.

ERIC: Diane.

DIANE: You shouldn't even be in this house.

ERIC: The door was open.

DIANE: There is an acre of private property between the road and that door.

ERIC: And very handsome property it is. Your apple trees are still in bloom, they've all gone by in the city. Nice house, too.

DIANE: So glad you approve.

ERIC: Strange that I've never seen it. I guess Henry only had his top-tier artists out to visit.

DIANE: No.

ERIC: No?

DIANE: This was his refuge. This is where he went to escape the whole crazy, needy lot of you.

ERIC: Sam's been here. He described the place to me.

DIANE: He's a neighbor, that's different.

ERIC: So just your rich clients, then.

DIANE: Maybe just the loyal ones.

ERIC: Loyal.

DIANE: I'm sorry, did I use an unfamiliar word? Loyal, L-O-Y-

ERIC: Loyalty can't afford to be blind. It's earned by good service.

DIANE: You were very well taken care of.

ERIC: Where would I be now if I'd stayed, with Henry . . . I'm sorry, by the way. I'm sorry about Henry. Truly.

DIANE: So sorry they were the first words out of your mouth.

ERIC: I sent a note, you never replied.

DIANE: Why are you here, Eric?

ERIC: You know damn well, why. If you didn't want me here, you could have avoided it with one phone call.

DIANE: I had nothing to say to you.

ERIC: Fine. Then you could simply have packed the pieces up and shipped them to me.

DIANE: Anything belonging to you was returned long ago.

ERIC: Not the four black paintings.

DIANE: The portraits, you mean?

ERIC: They're not portraits.

DIANE: Funny, they used to be. Odd how much a work can change, years after being completed.

ERIC: Just because a work is inspired by a living subject does not make it a portrait. Don't pretend to such simple-minded ideas.

DIANE: They don't belong to you.

ERIC: I made them.

DIANE: You made many things which no longer belong to you.

ERIC: For which I was compensated.

DIANE: You want money?

ERIC: I want what's mine. Your father knew those works were only for safekeeping.

DIANE: You didn't give them to Henry. You gave them to me.

ERIC: Never. You invented that and now you've convinced yourself it's true, but I never said it. We've been through all of this.

DIANE: That's right, we have. That's why I didn't return your calls.

ERIC: And the facts haven't changed. What do you think, that I'm just going to give up, that you can outlast me? The next step is lawyers. You understand that, I hope.

DIANE: I'd be pretty stupid if I didn't, since you've threatened it in every message.

ERIC: Is that what you want?

DIANE: You're too cheap to hire a lawyer.

ERIC: Helen's already found me one.

DIANE: Helen, of course. You just go from one nursemaid to another. Tell me, now that it doesn't matter anymore: Were you already sleeping with her before you left us?

ERIC: I am not sleeping with her.

DIANE: Really? And here I thought she slept with all her clients. She's clearly not the full-service provider you expected.

ERIC: Do you really want to be throwing rocks in that particular neighborhood?

DIANE: Oh, I assure you I have nothing on Helen. You were my sole mistake in that area. And my last.

ERIC: Why do you have to make it like this?

DIANE: Me? Why do I have to —

ERIC: People have affairs, they end, they move on.

DIANE: This is not about that.

ERIC: Then what the hell is it about?

DIANE: What you did to my father.

ERIC: I did not do anything to your father.

DIANE: Just broke his heart, that's all. Just destroyed his will to fight.

ERIC: I made a business decision. An artist has the right to make a change when his gallery can no longer place his work.

DIANE: An artist has a duty to know when his work has become inferior and repetitive, and to take a hard look inside himself.

ERIC: Interesting that you never made those critiques when they might have mattered.

DIANE: As if you would have listened.

ERIC: That's not the point, is it?

DIANE: You're right. I could see it happening and I said nothing. I was a coward. I didn't want to scare you away. Sue me.

ERIC: Give me my Goddamn paintings, Diane. (*He slams his hand down on the box, then sees it for the first time.*) What is this?

DIANE: Ashes.

ERIC: (*Backing away.*) That's not Henry, is it?

DIANE: He wanted to be scattered on the beach, at sunrise. Sunrises are beautiful out here, not that I've seen many. But he was always up before dawn, city or country. Drinking coffee while the world slept, calling his pals in London. Thinking about what he could do that day to help his artists.

ERIC: He did me a lot of good, I'd never say otherwise. He loved painters, not these idiots with their videos and shellacked cow intestines. I've missed him this past year. Missed both of you.

DIANE: How sweet.

ERIC: But he'd lost his touch, or maybe he was just tired. He only had time for Sam, Masako, fucking Reinhardt. I barely spoke to him those last few months.

DIANE: Because he knew I was taking care of you. Who sold your last half dozen pieces?

ERIC: It was his gallery.

DIANE: I did.

ERIC: I needed his attention, his approval.

DIANE: And I would have continued to look after you long after Henry was gone.

ERIC: It wasn't the same. I mean, I'm grateful, especially since it turns out you were selling work you clearly hated.

DIANE: That's not what I said.

ERIC: But how long ago were those sales?

DIANE: How many pieces has Helen sold for you?

ERIC: I hear Reinhardt left. Went to Gagosian.

DIANE: Good riddance.

ERIC: And Sam's thinking about it.

DIANE: Not that he's told me. But if it's true, at least he had the decency to wait until Henry died.

ERIC: So if I'd waited a year I'd be off the hook?

DIANE: No.

ERIC: Why?

DIANE: You don't listen. Because I was the one taking care of you.

ERIC: You see, this *is* about you and me. You're lying to yourself, using Henry as a shield.

DIANE: Get out of my house, Eric.

ERIC: Look, we all loved you, loved having you involved in our business. You were the strong right hand the old guy needed. But Henry . . . Henry was irreplaceable.

DIANE: Apparently not.

ERIC: *(Long pause.)* One piece.

DIANE: One piece of what?

ERIC: What you asked before. Helen sold one piece from the last show. And I haven't even been paid for it.

DIANE: Poor you.

ERIC: Made me wonder about leaving Henry, leaving you. It's always easier to blame someone else. I really thought this was strong stuff. I got rid of all of that blue and yellow I was using, all those bright colors and geometric shapes. Went back to the black and white, the semi-abstract forms.

DIANE: I saw the show.

ERIC: You did? Then you know where I'm going with this. Simple, rigorous, tough, it just poured out of me. Best work in years. And nobody bought it. Got three small, mediocre reviews. I was in a rage, you remember my rages?

DIANE: Yes.

ERIC: And then I walked through the gallery, right before they took the show down. Really looked at each piece. And it was all garbage. Empty canvases. At best, a memory of something good I'd once done, but not the thing itself. That's why I need the black paintings back. I haven't done anything like those since, but maybe they'll help me remember how.

DIANE: It doesn't work like that.

ERIC: How the hell would you know?

DIANE: They're creatures of the time in which you created them. They're dead to you now. What's good, what's real, lives in your fingers, in your muscle memory. In your instinct, if you could clear away all the expectations and bullshit.

ERIC: Maybe you're right.

DIANE: The paintings themselves would only be a burden to you.

ERIC: I still want them.

DIANE: Do you really? Is that really why you came?

ERIC: Why else?

DIANE: Maybe to say you were sorry, or that you made a mistake, or that you still . . .

ERIC: I'm sorry I hurt you. And I probably did make a mistake, but it's one I plan to live with.

DIANE: Well good for you.

ERIC: Can I have my paintings?

DIANE: Sure.

ERIC: Thank you. Thank you, Diane. This may sound inappropriate, but I'm going to ask anyway. I want to be there when you scatter Henry's ashes. It would mean a lot to me.

DIANE: Sorry. We scattered them yesterday morning. Just my sister, me, and Sam. It was a lovely moment.

ERIC: Then what's in the box?

DIANE: Your paintings. Your four black paintings. There's a note, too, I was about to send them to you.

ERIC: This is not even funny.

DIANE: They burned beautifully. You were the one to tell me there's no such thing as black paint, the artist chooses his dark pigments, and you can see it if you look closely. Black may be the absence of all light, but it's the presence of all color, yes? And I could see all of those colors in the flames, a jet of blue, of purple, a sudden burst of green. I know they're not portraits, but I could see my face in every one, black becoming rainbow fire, becoming ash. It was cleansing. I did it right out there on the patio, last night. You can still see the scorch marks.

ERIC: *(Rushing to the door and then stopping.)* You're lying. You would never do that to art, it's not in you.

DIANE: There's a bottom corner of one that survived. It's right on top, just open the flaps and see. Go ahead. A little courage is required in this life.

ERIC: No.

DIANE: Take the box, then. Open it at your leisure.

ERIC: I'll take everything you own. The gallery will collapse overnight when people hear about this.

DIANE: I'm closing the gallery, and moving back to London. My lawyers will know where to find me.

ERIC: How can you possibly justify this?

DIANE: Besides your killing my father? To set myself free. To set us both free. Someday you'll thank me.

ERIC: Someday you'll understand what you've done, and why.

DIANE: Don't forget your paintings.

ERIC: Keep them. They really do resemble you now. *(Exits.)*

DIANE: *(Staring at the box.)* Don't look at me like that. I had a right. He'll get over it. He gets over everything, that's his problem. Me, I can't let anything go, or anyone. *(Placing her hand on the box.)* But I will. Tomorrow, at sunrise.

END OF PLAY

If I Could Paint the Rain

ROSARY HARTEL O'NEILL

CHARACTERS
ROOSTER
MONICA

SETTING
The dayroom of a Garden District mansion, New Orleans, Louisiana

. . .

The dayroom of a Garden District mansion, New Orleans, Louisiana. The not-too-distant present. A spacious room, with one door on the left wall, and two on the right. In the center stands a table, with chairs round it: sketch-pads, brushes, and paints are lying on the table. Downstage, left is a window and near it a chair with a drawing table. In the right wall is a door that leads into a gloomy garden shrouded in steady rain. There is a luxuriously cush-ioned daybed with an empty birdcage like a Chinese house. Vivid landscape paintings are placed about. The effect is of a boy's dream, the actual furniture being less important than the wonder created.
Sound: It is raining quietly, one of those late-afternoon showers that New Orleans is famous for. Rooster Dubonnet, a young man, twenties, dark-haired, gaunt, almost emaciated, lies in bed in silk pajamas. A painter who has pushed himself beyond reasonable limits. He is critically ill from cancer. The disease gives him a distinct nonchalance, the charm of the damned. If he were not so sick and pasty-looking, he could be handsome with strong features, thick hair, and broad shoulders. Even so, there are kindness and nobility in his face.

ROOSTER: I'm cold. Maybe the rain makes me that way. It's full of emptiness. Cold blue in the morning, bright blue at noon and intense Italiante blue in the late afternoon. The walls soak up the rain. There is vermilion in the shadows, violet in the gray. Like the sound of everything that's there, that I try to paint. When you are inside the rain, there's luminosity. I want images that have the density of rain. Nature does it easily. When you try to copy it, it's gone. Rain's not easily captured. It's the pink lie, the last little thing that crawled out of Pandora's box with all her colors. If I could paint rain the way it is, thick and smelling of oak leaves, I could figure life out.

(Rooster closes his eyes. Monica Falcon, a stunning nurse, twenties, arrives. Delicate features match her gentleness: fine skin, graceful hands, hair that tum-bles about her face. She is dressed simply but impeccably and holds a satchel

under her arm. She pauses at the doorway, removing her cape and looking about in the house.)

MONICA: Hello, hello . . . anyone there? I'm Monica Falcon, the new nurse.

ROOSTER: What? *(Calls out.)* Ma.

MONICA: *(Puts thermometer in his mouth.)* Are you in pain?

ROOSTER: No.

(He pulls out the thermometer, leans to an intercom.)

MONICA: You sounded as if you were in pain.

ROOSTER: *(Into the intercom.)* Ma, pick up.

MONICA: Everyone's gone.

ROOSTER: Unlikely.

(Into the intercom.)

Pick up, I said.

MONICA: The house echoes quiet.

ROOSTER: *(Into the intercom.)* Ma. They sent a woman.

MONICA: You've a wonderful house . . .

ROOSTER: *(Into the intercom.)* I asked for a male nurse.

MONICA: It's like a hotel.

ROOSTER: *(Into the intercom.)* You're not my guest. I'm not lying about half-dressed with a woman.

(Monica checks about for lights.)

ROOSTER: Don't.

MONICA: Do you live in darkness?

ROOSTER: Best way to survive in the Garden District.

MONICA: *(Looks at her feet.)* These shoes looked good before I walked through water.

ROOSTER: Click your heels and go back to Oz.

MONICA: We can catch the last rays of the sun.

ROOSTER: You're not staying.

(He sits up, reaches for his robe, but is still weak and has to breathe a few moments. She looks out the window. He reaches for the phone.)

MONICA: The light feels good. Cold bracing sunshine, right behind the rain. That'll keep you awake.

ROOSTER: *(Into the receiver.)* Is this the Parker Agency?

MONICA: I love a bright afternoon sky.

ROOSTER: This is Rooster Dubonnet. I requested a male nurse.

MONICA: *(Reaches for the phone.)* Give me that.

ROOSTER: *(Stretches phone away, panting, talks into it.)* I'm not paying for this woman.

MONICA: What do you have against women?

ROOSTER: *(Into the phone.)* I was nice to those rejects you sent. She can't be the only nurse who'll come.

MONICA: *(Takes out a blood pressure kit.)* I'll take your blood pressure.

ROOSTER: *(Into the phone.)* You said you had 200 nurses.

(Into the phone.)

I don't want this woman.

(Into the phone.)

Tell her to leave.

MONICA: *(Takes phone, speaks into it.)* Everybody's fine.

(Hangs up. To Rooster.)

One, two, three . . . up.

(Rooster sits up, very weak, wraps his robe limply over his silk pajamas.)

ROOSTER: Stay away. I'm warning you.

MONICA: Let me help you to that chair.

ROOSTER: I'm calling the police.

(He reaches for the phone, but she grabs it and puts it in her pocket.)

MONICA: I'll change those sheets.

(He stumbles to his feet. He is panting for breath, totters, and grasps onto furniture. He stops for a second. She watches him from the corner of her eyes and goes to make the bed.)

MONICA: You can do it?

ROOSTER: I can do it.

(He presses a hand alarm, which blares. They struggle for the alarm. She pushes it off.)

MONICA: What's that? Turn it off.

ROOSTER: Not likely.

MONICA: Give it over.

ROOSTER: No.

MONICA: *(Pulls alarm from his fist.)* You think you can get rid of me?

ROOSTER: You're the roughest . . .

MONICA: My landlord's evicted me.

ROOSTER: Toughest . . .

MONICA: Called me at five AM.

ROOSTER: This is not a hotel.

MONICA: I've no friends or relatives here.

ROOSTER: That's the first good news about you.

MONICA: I'd like to help.

(He walks, but stumbles. She calls out as he moves cautiously along.)

Take my arm!

ROOSTER: I'm not some bag you can carry around.

MONICA: Can you get to that door?

ROOSTER: Uh-huh. If I push myself I can.

(He walks carefully. Reaching the door, he rests his head back, then turns and sets off a strobe light siren. She runs over. They struggle for it.)

MONICA: You crazy . . .

ROOSTER: You want to hear the sound of a siren . . .

MONICA: Out of my way!

ROOSTER: I'm weak, but I can do it.

MONICA: Stop. Nobody's going to bail me out.

(She turns the siren off. He staggers to a chair and leans over the back, coughing.)

MONICA: Have you had anything to eat? Or drink?

ROOSTER: Not today.

MONICA: (Hands him water.) Take a few sips.

ROOSTER: No, thanks. Have you ever heard of the nurse who poisons the emperor? This emperor so feared assassination, he only ate ripe figs from a tree.

MONICA: Drink.

ROOSTER: In the night, his nurse injected them with poison.

MONICA: Just . . .

ROOSTER: In the morning, the emperor ate one and died.

(He drinks a little, then pours water on a plant. She speaks continuously, overlapping him.)

MONICA: Since you won't let me help you, may I ask you some questions?

ROOSTER: What's that?

MONICA: I'm studying astrology . . . on the side.

ROOSTER: It's amateur night in Dixie.

MONICA: I looked you up. You've got a tenth house, Pluto in Leo.

ROOSTER: Fortune-tellers. They're everything I'm running from —

MONICA: Which means you're gifted . . .

ROOSTER: (Breathing fast.) The whole spectre of charlatans —

MONICA: At being able to . . .

ROOSTER: That haunt artists' history.

MONICA: Translate archetypal energy . . .

ROOSTER: I'm three times more likely to die from the flu . . .

MONICA: Through the power of the personal image . . .

ROOSTER: Than to speak to a student astrologer. Y'all are the psychos of the science profession.

MONICA: Think you can get in that chair?

ROOSTER: Uh-huh. If I'm careful, I can.

MONICA: I know you're a famous artist from a well-to-do family . . .

ROOSTER: Why do people pursue me?

MONICA: May I ask you some questions? It would make my job easier.

ROOSTER: You haven't a job with me.

MONICA: You're so . . .

ROOSTER: Difficult? Some artists don't do interviews, and thank God they don't do them. I don't want to be the entertainment.

MONICA: And you're not.

(Rooster rises with effort, crosses to the birdcage, whistles "Dixie.")

ROOSTER: My parrot, Commander Butler, just flew in.

MONICA: Where?

ROOSTER: He died but sometimes he visits. He's my very special house ghost. The two things Butler does best are scream, "Where's the maid?" and whistle, "Dixie." Calling the maid is so passé.

(Pause.)

You think I'm crazy.

MONICA: No. What's your diagnosis?

ROOSTER: I belong to the National Caged Bird Society . . .

MONICA: Your symptoms?

ROOSTER: But I couldn't make that bird talk.

MONICA: How long have . . .

ROOSTER: Butler's a Southerner from French aristocrats . . .

MONICA: You been sick?

ROOSTER: He was bred by a gentleman who kept his plantation up river. One difference between Butler and me. He's dead and I'm alive. But I'll be flying off soon.

(Pause.)

Are you from the South?

MONICA: Delaware.

ROOSTER: Y'all like to eat on paper plates in halls covered with graffiti. What do you have going for you? That's what I want to know.

MONICA: My husband was from Jackson.

ROOSTER: There's a touch of Mississippi in your family? What does Mr. Falcon do without you?

MONICA: My . . . I . . . Oh Lord . . . I mustn't let . . . Where're my Kleenex? You think I'd be here if I . . .

ROOSTER: Take my handkerchief.

(She does.)

Don't start the sadness machine.

MONICA: It happens frequently. I'm so tired, and broke. It's not professional. I don't want to be so emotional. Your bed is ready.

(Rain pours around the sides of the room. She removes the thermometer, writes something on her chart. He pulls a sketchpad from behind a seat.)

ROOSTER: I've not stopped painting because I wanted to. This morning I said to myself, I'm going to paint, if my energy holds out . . . Soon as it's warm and the sun's shining . . .

MONICA: Well?

(Rain begins whistling around. He rubs the armrests.)

ROOSTER: My energy didn't hold out . . . Listen to that rain blowing round outside.

MONICA: It sounds neighborly.

ROOSTER: Coming right through the sun.

MONICA: I love to hear it when I'm inside.

ROOSTER: Oh, but it's cold walking into the rain when you have to.

(Begins to shiver.)

Look at me shake, will you? The thought of rain and I start to shiver.

MONICA: Try to nap. Would you like another blanket?

(He lies back slowly. She covers him.)

ROOSTER: That does feel good.

MONICA: I told you.

(He has closed his eyes and gone to sleep. Monica watches over him as the lights are brought down. The lights come up.)

END OF PLAY

A Simple Snow

ELAINE ROMERO

A Simple Snow was written during the Artist Residency Program at the Cornucopia Art Center in Lanesboro, Minnesota.

CHARACTERS

ALICE: a woman who has found herself in a new environment
MAN: he drives a carriage

TIME

Anytime

PLACE

A snowy place

SETTING

A carriage in the snow. A frozen body lies nearby.

•   •   •

A carriage in the snow. Man whips the horses. They hit a pothole. Woman loses her balance.

MAN: Hold on.

WOMAN: I don't know if it's your driving or not, but there seems to be a pothole every five seconds.

MAN: It's not my driving.

WOMAN: I guess I'm used to walking.

Thank you. Thank you for the lift.

MAN: You didn't have any baggage?

Where are you coming from?

I understand. I've taken a few like you.

WOMAN: What're you saying, sir?

MAN: People coming from nowhere.

WOMAN: Well, I'd just rather not talk about it. My employer, well, he's very important. Well, I've promised to protect his identity.

(They hit another pothole. The snow falls all at once.)

Would you watch your driving?

I swear a child is in charge of this carriage.

MAN: It's just Christmas. It shakes things up. Inside people.

The holidays make people weep.

WOMAN: Not me. I'm frozen here. I would have died out there. I'm sorry for the complaints. My employer — well, you see, he died. Rather sudden. Frozen in the snow.

MAN: I'm sorry.

WOMAN: I found him last night. Myself. So, you see, I'm a little bit out of sorts. He didn't leave any provisions . . . in his will. My employer.

(She starts to cry.)

MAN: Doesn't sound as if he was just an employer.

WOMAN: Are you accusing me of some sort of disgrace?

MAN: No, ma'am.

(The snow falls. Another pothole.)

WOMAN: This is just a shaky world we live in. Earthquakes every few minutes. People freezing in the snow. Life has been thrown asunder.

See, I walked through a tunnel. It started in London or in New York City. I had said good-bye to the world. I had kissed the city good-bye, turned on my heel and put my back to it. Betrayed it like that.

And then, I landed here — in the land of unsettled earth. And I met my employer. He never said much. Nothing really. Not much could move him, but then, most bosses are like that. Quiet and stern. Don't say much. And I adorned him with suits and clothes, with neckties and cigars. It seemed a paycheck might not come, but he was good to me. Never spoke a harsh word . . . never spoke a word. And then I touched him and he was hard like he'd frozen in the night. Like the blood had stopped coursing through his veins — he was so important. But I left the city. Did I say? I left the dress shop. I stopped sweeping in the morning, and I was wrong. I was wrong to love whom I loved. I don't think he knew. My minister. And his wife. I loved them both. In a different way. I loved them both so much. This whole thing unnerves me. This tremor in my heart shakes my hands.

I had a cranberry cake that I'd made for them and their children. I am contemptible. And I was walking through the snow on my way to them. And I tripped, or actually, fell through one of those holes in the street. *(Realizing where.)* In New York City. And I landed, in this strange place where men drive carriages or don't speak for days on end, or pay you for services rendered because their minds are preoccupied with other worlds. But I'm not bitter.

I landed here.

MAN: Well, I've been looking for someone to love. I mean, driving in the snow every day from town to town, hitting potholes I cannot see with my hollow eyes, has left me disoriented in this shaky world.

WOMAN: Ever since I left New York. Ever since I was Alice, in the rabbit hole, I just haven't been the same.

(She sneezes.)

MAN: You could join me. On this carriage. We could hold hands. Sometimes the snow catches the moonlight and the job becomes very pretty.

(Woman looks off the side of the carriage.)

WOMAN: Why, that's my employer.

(Woman tries to crawl off the moving carriage.)

MAN: Watch it, miss.

WOMAN: Could you stop this thing?

MAN: I'm sorry. It seems to have a mind of its own.

WOMAN: You could slow down for a lady.

MAN: I apologize, ma'am.

I believe it is has stopped, ma'am.

(Woman crawls down the side of the carriage.)

WOMAN: That's my employer. I'm beginning to believe, sir, that you have been taking me in a circle 'round and 'round. You have duped me into believing that I am making progress when I am making none.

MAN: No, ma'am. This here is the standstill world. That's where you landed when you left yours.

(Man hits a pothole, but she shakes though she is not on the carriage. Her arms are outstretched as she strives to balance herself.)

WOMAN: Get off that carriage, sir. I demand it.

MAN: It's my job. Hands on reins. Horses in place. Trees standing next to me. Frozen body at my side.

WOMAN: Remove your hands.

MAN: Sorry, can't oblige.

(She crosses to him and pounds on him, realizing he is frozen.)

WOMAN: If you weren't talking, I'd assume you were dead.

MAN: Sorry to disappoint. I've offered you my world. The seat next to me, in this, my fine carriage.

(She falls to her knees. She starts trying to get up.)

WOMAN: What is this place?

What is it?

MAN: I don't know. You claim to have fallen down the hole. Do you remember?

(Woman runs to the edge of the world, discovering the glass dome of the snow globe. She runs her hands up the curvature of the space.)

WOMAN: Sir, sir. It feels hard. Like glass.

(Their world is shaken again. She presses her eyes against the glass.)

It's flesh. Very *large* flesh. Could it be the hand of God is revealed to me in my sorrow? Did he discover my love for the preacher and encase me as punishment? How cruel is God to those with hearts as large as mine?

(Woman lands on her bum.)

Oh, no. A world that shakes. A world with endless snow. A world run as if in the hands of a child. I'm beginning to suspect I'm captive here.

(She puts her eyes against the glass.)

Oh, my, it's Christmas. I see the tree and the lights. The angel at the tree's tip hangs at a precarious angle and I want to catch her. I see the fire and the unwrapped gifts. I see the minister and his wife. They're eating cranberry cake and drinking Christmas wine.

Why, the last time I saw him, I fell down that hole. In the city. The city of New York. Outside of Macy's, it was. The whole place was lit up for Christmas. And I could hear the carolers in the background. They sang beautifully as I lay there — dying.

Sir, I believe I died.

Sir, I think I know where I've landed. I've come to understand the mystery of the afterlife.

See, on my way, to their apartment, I stopped at Macy's and I looked at those snowy displays. They had snowmen and Santa and my city in the winter, and they had the sweetest one I'd ever seen. A man and a carriage. And I willed myself there to that simple life. In the snow. I wished myself there. When I died.

MAN: Would you like to join me, miss?

WOMAN: Sir, it seems you've missed my startling revelation.

Sir, did you used to be real?

MAN: This is the life I've always known.

WOMAN: My employer?

MAN: He never did move though I saw you adorned him.

WOMAN: What a macabre scene for a snowy display. A dead man.

MAN: You wished yourself here.

WOMAN: I would like it, sir. But first give me a chance to watch the world I once knew as if I could live there without pain.

(She does.)

It's the minister. He is holding his wife. On Christmas.

(She starts to cry.)

I believe, sir, that I am capable of the deepest kind of love. Steadfast love. They are beautiful. Together.

(She sees the son.)

Oh, here he comes.

(He shakes their world.)

I wonder what will happen when he forgets about us, when Christmas is over and we are no longer the latest toy.

MAN: Sometimes the moonlight hits the snow and the job can be very pretty.

WOMAN: Will you talk to me forever, sir?

Maybe, if you whip your horses hard enough, we could burst through the glass someday. Make ourselves known.

MAN: Maybe.

(She goes back and sits beside him.)

WOMAN: I am grateful. For the company in this ordinary life.

MAN: I am, too, ma'am.

WOMAN: If you stopped . . . your job, we could kiss.

(She grabs his hands.)

MAN: Hands on the reins.

WOMAN: I heard about the frog prince once. The princess kissed him and it made him real.

(She kisses his cheek. He releases the reins and turns.)

MAN: What is this?

What is this I feel?

WOMAN: Will you hold me now?

(He does.)

You are the most handsome man. The handsome man from the Christmas display at Macy's. The man from the snow globe.

(She puts her arms around him.)

MAN: Oh, my, what is this I feel?

(He shivers.)

WOMAN: It's cold. You are in the snow.

May I kiss you?

(She does.)

MAN: I feel as if . . .

WOMAN: As if you're alive.

Come, I'll show you a whole new world.

(He gets off the carriage with her. She leads him to the back of the carriage.)
We will make love. Oh, don't blush. It's very nice. I will rub my body against yours.

MAN: Oh, my.

WOMAN: And when we're done. When I've shown you the most marvelous part of life, we will burst our way out of the glass. Out into the world once mine and lost.

(The world shakes. She moves to the edge of the world.)
It's the little boy. He's picked us up.

(They tumble.)
And dropped us.

(She kicks the glass.)
But it didn't break.

MAN: Come here, my love, and show me the most wonderful part of life. I am eager to experience it. And when we are done, we will burst into your old world with renewed vigor.

WOMAN: Or we could stay inside and make love forever.

MAN: That is too pleasant a thought though I've never experienced it. My body screams out for your flesh. You've carnalized me!

WOMAN: We could spend our lives discovering each other's bodies. The feel of your legs and chest, the passion of your kiss.

MAN: I am most eager to get started, ma'am.

WOMAN: Alice. Like the looking glass.

MAN: Alice.

WOMAN: And what is your name?

MAN: I have none.

WOMAN: You're Clyde. Your name is Clyde. Clyde, are you ready to learn the most marvelous part of life?
(She takes his hand and moves him to the back of the carriage. This time it shakes, not from the hand of the child, but because of their lovemaking.)

MAN: *(Offstage.)* To think I've only known the front of this carriage when the back held such earthly delights.

WOMAN: *(Offstage.)* I do love you, Clyde, more than that minister and his wife. Clyde. Clyde, the world holds many difficult things. Hunger and starvation when we could just stay frozen here, as if in a pause.

MAN: *(Offstage.)* We could.

WOMAN: *(Offstage.)* Or we could brave it. We could brave empty bellies, employment, disappointment, and joy. Will you? Will you bear the burden of time with me?
(They emerge from the carriage disheveled and content. She takes him to the edge of the world.)
Here it is. The edge of the world. See, the Christmas lights and the trees. One. Two. Three. Kick. One, two, three . . . kick. One, two, three . . . kick. It's useless. The glass that encases us is too strong.
(He points to the carriage.)

MAN: I would like to make love again.

WOMAN: *(With humor.)* You are alive.

MAN: I'd like that.

WOMAN: You are my companion.

MAN: Yes.

WOMAN: Will you help me return to the world someday?

MAN: Let's go back to the carriage, and soon they will leave.

(They return.)

The most wonderful part of life is here for the taking.

WOMAN: But I'm hungry. And my cranberry cake looks moist and sweet.

MAN: I've seen a glimpse of your world and I think I prefer ours.

WOMAN: You're on display. You're a trinket easily forgotten or packed away in an attic.

MAN: The most wonderful part of life is here for the taking.

WOMAN: You are lovely. Perfect. What I always dreamed of. Perhaps I've died and gone to a realm beyond Earth.

MAN: Perhaps.

(They kiss.)

WOMAN: I could kiss you forever.

MAN: You will.

WOMAN: No, we must burst out of this place with the force of our will. Will you come with me? Do you dare?

(The world shakes. The snow falls. They both teeter. They stand looking at each other from far apart. She walks forward through the glass back into the real world. He returns to his carriage and takes his seat.)

END OF PLAY

Horticultural Therapy

GEORGE SAUER

The first production of *Horticultural Therapy* was by The
Turnip Theatre Company and the American Globe Theatre
with Erick Herrscher as Director and with the
following cast: Brian Patacca (Howard) and
Kate Tellers (Renee).

CHARACTERS
RENEE: female
HOWARD: male, her husband

SETTING
A condo in New York City

TIME
The present

•   •   •

Setting: An empty stage. At Rise: Howard holds a notice.

HOWARD: Have you seen this?
RENEE: Ya. What's with posting notices in the lobby? This is a co-op not a dormitory.
HOWARD: Are you going to answer it?
RENEE: I haven't decided yet.
HOWARD: But it says it's important to contact her. *Important* highlighted in pink.
RENEE: If it was that important, the note should explain why.
HOWARD: Maybe we were exposed to something.
RENEE: Exposed to something? It was a dead plant!
HOWARD: We don't know that.
RENEE: Excuse me?
HOWARD: Well, we don't know that much about horticulture. We live in a condo in the middle of Manhattan.
RENEE: You don't need to live in a cornfield in friggin' Iowa to know when a plant is dead.
HOWARD: But it could still be toxic.
RENEE: Then what the hell was it doing in a pot on the roof deck?
HOWARD: Maybe in its dead form it's toxic. Like isn't tapioca made from a root and if you don't beat out all the poison it can be deadly?
RENEE: What are you talking about?
HOWARD: Tapioca. You know the pudding?
RENEE: That they give old people in nursing homes?
HOWARD: Well, they serve it in restaurants too.
RENEE: Not any restaurants we go to.
HOWARD: My point is things can take different forms in nature. What looks harmless may actually not be.

RENEE: You're making too much of this note. Just ignore it.
  (Renee grabs note and crumples it.)

•

(Howard holds another notice.)
HOWARD: You were up there again weren't you?
RENEE: Up where?
  (Renee grabs note and crumples it.)

•

(Howard holds another notice.)
HOWARD: Did you read this!
RENEE: Yes.
HOWARD: She knows the latin name for the plant you removed!
RENEE: That "I" removed?
HOWARD: I'm telling you, we're way over our heads here. Why couldn't you just let it end?
RENEE: My question is how does she know now to slip the notes under our door?
  (Renee grabs note and crumples it.)

•

(Howard holds another notice.)
HOWARD: What is this?
RENEE: It's a notice. They should look familiar by now.
HOWARD: Did you make it?
RENEE: Why do you think that?
HOWARD: Well it is in your handwriting.
RENEE: I thought it gave a more personal touch than using the computer.
HOWARD: Why are you doing this?
RENEE: I'm just questioning whether plants belong on the roof. I mean think of it, "roof garden"
  Who came up with the idea? Do plants even want to be that high-up? That close to the sun? I'm just asking questions.
HOWARD: This is insane!
  (Howard crumples notice.)

(Howard holds another notice.)

HOWARD: All right. All right. I called her. I had to. You can't believe what they're saying in the lobby. In the elevator. In the laundry room. The accusations. So, I called her. Her name is Nina. Apparently she designs roof gardens. We met her once in fact. Remember when we were sitting on the roof and this woman, Nina, had invited some people who had kids her daughter's age for a playgroup and you wouldn't give up your seat so one of the parents had to stand? Not that that incident had anything to do with all of this. I don't think Nina even made the association.

RENEE: Bullshit!

HOWARD: At any rate, apparently the plant you, we removed was very rare.

RENEE: Oh, I see. Not just rare, but *very* rare.

HOWARD: I'm just quoting her.

RENEE: Did you mention it was dead?

HOWARD: We didn't really get into —

RENEE: That would be a "no." So thanks to us this species is now extinct. Is that it?

HOWARD: Again we didn't get into the specifics of all that.

RENEE: So, what did she want?

HOWARD: Well, I think she was concerned that we might dig up more plants.

RENEE: I haven't decided yet.

HOWARD: Well, I think the thrust of the meeting was that she advised against doing that.

RENEE: So she has supreme authority over the roof garden?

HOWARD: Well that is her profession and she did donate all the plants.

RENEE: If she is what she claims she is, I'm sure she skims them from other projects.

HOWARD: She wanted to have her say so I listened.

RENEE: Where did this take place?

HOWARD: What?

RENEE: This conversation. Over the phone?

HOWARD: No. I , ah, met her for coffee.

RENEE: Oh? Did you pay?

HOWARD: Well, ya. It was just coffee . . . and danish.

RENEE: No. For the plant. Did you offer to pay for the plant?

HOWARD: I gave her one hundred dollars. We killed a rare plant. A very rare plant. One hundred dollars seemed appropriate.

RENEE: Appropriate? You betrayed me. Is that appropriate?

HOWARD: Renee!! At least it's over.

RENEE: What makes you think that?

(Howard crumbles note.)

•

(Howard holds another notice.)

HOWARD: Why are you doing this?

RENEE: Doing what?

HOWARD: What! This insane horticultural jihad!!

RENEE: I have no idea what you're talking about.

HOWARD: Don't you think I see you? Walking down the street pulling plants out of flower boxes!

RENEE: Oh that? I'm dead-heading them.

HOWARD: What kind of term is that?

RENEE: Didn't Nina explain that to you? It's the horticultural term for removing dead flowers so new blossoms can form.

HOWARD: You pull plants up by their roots!!

RENEE: I practice an extreme form of dead-heading.

HOWARD: And someone in the elevator said they saw you attack that tree by the front entrance with a hammer!

RENEE: I was trying to stimulate sap flow.

HOWARD: I'm calling someone.

RENEE: Who? The police? I want to hear that phone conversation.

HOWARD: Renee, new notices are going up in the lobby!

RENEE: Why are you following me? Did your friend Nina put you up to it?

(Renee grabs notice and crumples it.)

•

(Howard holds another notice.)

HOWARD: I'd like you to meet with Nina.

RENEE: Oh, really?

HOWARD: She wants to talk to you.

RENEE: So?

HOWARD: You see, it turns out, she also does something called "horticultural therapy."

RENEE: Is that like beating someone with a stick?

HOWARD: No. It's about integrating people with horticulture. Nina feels that city dwellers develop hostile feelings toward plants because they seldom come into contact with them in their natural state. Nina is a pioneer in the field.

RENEE: Somehow I guessed that.

HOWARD: She sent you this flier.

RENEE: You know for someone who is so fond of trees, she sure doesn't mind turning them into paper.

HOWARD: I think it's recycled. Don't crumple it! Please. Just meet with her. What harm can come from it?

RENEE: OK. Sure. What the hell.

As long as I can bring my hammer.

(Renee neatly folds notice.)

•

(Renee hands Howard a notice.)

HOWARD: Another notice?

RENEE: It's Nina's idea.

HOWARD: Oh?

RENEE: It's a plant playgroup that I'm helping to organize.

HOWARD: For kids?

RENEE: No. Adults.

HOWARD: And you do what, exactly?

RENEE: Play with plants. We hold them. We touch them. We talk to them. It's very calming.

HOWARD: You can't be serious!

RENEE: Very.

(Renee grabs back notice.)

•

(Howard holds another notice.)

HOWARD: What's this?

RENEE: It's my new address.

HOWARD: Business?

RENEE: No. My new residence.

HOWARD: What? Where are you going?

RENEE: Costa Rica.

HOWARD: Costa Rica!

RENEE: To the rain forest. Apparently my case is so severe, I need total submersion in an environment that is predominately vegetation.

HOWARD: Couldn't you just take daily walks in Central Park?

RENEE: Nina says no.

HOWARD: Or we could go camping for a week in the White Mountains.

RENEE: Nina says no.

HOWARD: What! Does Nina have supreme authority over our lives.

RENEE: Well, she is my therapist. What's the point of my seeing her if I don't follow her advice?

HOWARD: How long will you be gone?

RENEE: At least a year.

HOWARD: A year!

RENEE: Or longer.

HOWARD: What am I supposed to do for a year?

RENEE: Be supportive.

HOWARD: Fuck being supportive!

RENEE: Nina warned me you might react this way.

HOWARD: Oh, fuck Nina!

(Howard crumples notice.)

•

(Howard and Renee each hold notices.)

RENEE: Dear Howard.

HOWARD: Dear Renee.

RENEE: It seems ages since I've written.

HOWARD: I haven't heard from you for months.

RENEE: The sugar cane harvest is the best in years and the workday is very long.

HOWARD: One of our neighbors slipped on a patch of ice and toppled off the roof so our roof garden is closed.

RENEE: I miss the landscape of buildings, lights, and energy.

HOWARD: I miss our potted plants.

RENEE: But only for a moment.

HOWARD: But only for a moment. Life here goes on.

RENEE: No. Life here grows on.

You must come sometime for a visit.

HOWARD: Nina sends her love.

(Howard and Renee crumple their notices.)

END OF PLAY

Outcome

S. W. SENEK

This play was originally performed in the 2003 Palm Springs National Short Play Festival at Playwrights' Circle in Palm Springs, California. It was directed by Eric Olson. The cast was as follows: Bob — Stephen Gergely; Lisa — Paige Thompson. This play was later performed at the 2004 New York Fifteen Minute Play Festival at the American Globe Theatre in Manhattan. It was directed by S. W. Senek. The cast was as follows: Bob — Joel Stigliano; Lisa — Kacey Durbin.

CHARACTERS
LISA
BOB

SETTING
In a bathroom somewhere in northern New Jersey

TIME
Morning

• • •

Lisa and Bob stand in front of the sink. Lisa clutches the results of a home-pregnancy test in her hand. Neither Bob nor Lisa has looked. They give each other an assuring smile.

LISA: Ready?

BOB: Ready. *(Beat. Snap change: He begins to speak his conscience to the audience.)* Oh my God.

LISA: *(Snap change: She begins to speak her conscience to the audience.)* Oh my God.

BOB: This is it.

LISA: The moment —

BOB: A —

LISA: Our life could change.

BOB: A —

LISA: He can't say it.

BOB: *(Encouraging himself.)* I can say it.

LISA: He *thinks* he can say it.

BOB: I *know* I can say it.

LISA: He can't.

BOB: Of course I can *(Deep breath. He tries to say it. Dejected exhale.)* I can't say it.

LISA: *I* can say it.

BOB: Look at her beaming, *she* can say it.

LISA: Pregnancy test —

BOB: She's just waiting to see the results.

LISA: *(Starts to bring the test up to see but stops.)* I can't look yet —

BOB: Is she? Isn't she? I can't take suspense. Suspense makes my skin itch. *(He scratches.)*

LISA: God, he's itching — he's full of suspense.

BOB: Suspense has filled me.

LISA: He's suspenseful.

BOB: I'm itching with suspense.

LISA: It's all about symbols on a little stick.

BOB: I wonder what they used before the stick. Leaves? Leaves are very important in some cultures. Some people still choose leaves over toilet paper.

LISA: A line through a circle represents a baby.

BOB: What do the symbols mean?

LISA: *(Trying to let it sink in.)* "Baby."

BOB: Circles, lines, squares, dots — the big dipper! I could never find the big dipper.

LISA: "Baby." *(Assuring.)* Saying it makes it real.

BOB: "Baby." *(Worried.)* Sounds too real.

LISA: *(Tries to believe the possibility of it.)* "Baby."

BOB AND LISA: Oh God.

BOB: What were we thinking?

LISA: It was so right at the time.

BOB: I mean, there she was saying "I want it." It was my obligation.

LISA: He wanted it — he begged me. "Please!" I hate to see him beg.

BOB: She could have used the old — "I'm feeling sick" line. I wouldn't have touched her.

LISA: I should've told him I was sick. He has this thing about germs.

BOB: Doorknobs. *(He pulls out a hanky.)* I can't touch doorknobs without my hanky.

LISA: The hanky. He takes it everywhere — to restaurants to hold his utensils. Our wedding, to put my ring on. Is that how he'll hold the baby?

BOB: At our wedding, the whole family kept telling us, "Have children!" Children. How does one think with children around?

LISA: "Baby." We just moved in. I haven't found an appropriate place for my antique ceramic thimble collection gathered from Finland.

BOB: We moved here less than a year ago. I don't even have my piano set up exactly where I want it. I'm very particular. It can take up to three years to find the right spot. There has to be just enough light.

LISA: I'm a real estate agent, not a mother.

BOB: Definitely not enough light — I've spent hours not playing but sitting.

LISA: How will I juggle a career and a baby?

BOB: How will I compose? I must have complete silence. There won't be silence — that and the light. Did I mention I get very tense with poor lighting?

LISA: "Oh, this is a perfect three bedroom, one-and-a-half-bath house complete with a — whoop — time to breast-feed. Excuse me while I whip my left breast out. So do you like it? *(Beat.)* The house, not my breast."

BOB: I'll have to play children's songs. I hate children's songs. It'll be hours of "Play it again, Daddy — again — again!"

LISA: It'll be countless arguments of *(Looks at Bob.)* "You take the kid."

BOB: *(To Lisa.)* No.

LISA: Yes, you take it.

BOB: No.

LISA: I can't — *(To the audience.)* I can't do this!

BOB: *(To the audience.)* I know this sounds a little selfish but . . . what about sex?

LISA: Look at him. He's thinking about sex.

BOB: Oh, damn, I can see her thinking about me thinking about sex. I'll think of other things.

LISA: I can see right though him.

BOB: I will put my shield up! *(Pantomimes pulling up his large shield. Stands proud like a superhero.)* She'll have no idea what I'm thinking now!

LISA: He's going into his "shield" phase. *(Bob stares at her.)* He's staring at me.

BOB: Oh God.

LISA: He's imagining me being huge.

BOB: She'll be huge.

LISA: He's thinking about sex again.

BOB: *(The thought of having sex with a very pregnant wife. Look of distaste.)* Ugh.

LISA: It's a beautiful thing.

BOB: If it were so beautiful, all adult magazines would go pregnant. It's an acquired taste.

LISA: It's natural. From the second you put on weight, you glow and — oh, no — this can't be. I spent countless hours on the exercise machines, doing weights, aerobics. He sabotaged me!

BOB: I read somewhere this is when women want sex the most.

LISA: We'll see if he'll like sex with me now!

BOB: I mean the kid will be right there.

LISA: We can still be intimate.

BOB: All three of us?

LISA: It's normal.

BOB: I have enough trouble being naked alone.

LISA: Of course Bob isn't normal. Take texture and food.

BOB: I'm particular — really.

LISA: If it doesn't feel right in his mouth, forget it.

BOB: Example, last night, Lisa made a Reuben casserole.

LISA: I made Reuben casserole. He took one bite.

BOB: I made an effort. I took several bites.

LISA: One bite.

BOB: We have unusually large forks.

LISA: He shoved it aside. I mean, he likes Reuben sandwiches.

BOB: Reuben sandwiches were not meant to be mashed into a pile known as a casserole. *(Ponder.)* God — no sex for nine months.

LISA: Maybe this will bring us closer.

BOB: This will put distance between us. She'll want to talk more.

LISA: Bob and I should talk more.

BOB: I'll take up a hobby — something to get me out of talking.

LISA: I remember when we met.

BOB: I remember meeting her — after one of my gigs.

LISA: We talked all night.

BOB: She would not shut up. All she could talk about was the apartments she showed that day.

LISA: So he kissed me.

BOB: I kissed her to shut her up. Oh, God, what if it runs in the genes. I like a good night's sleep.

LISA: I'll never sleep again.

BOB: Did I mention anything about my piano and lighting? It has to be perfect — like my sleep.

LISA: I must have at least ten hours sleep.

BOB: Is she going to expect me to get up in the middle of the night? What the hell can I do? I don't have any milk. Do I? *(He looks at himself in a mirror.)*

LISA: I knew it, he has breast envy.

BOB: *(Freezes.)* I should stop. *(Stops looking at himself.)* She'll think I have breast envy. *(Beat.)* OK, a little — but how can I contribute in the middle of the night?

LISA: He thinks he won't get up in the middle of the night.

BOB: I won't wake up. I'll block it all out.

LISA: It's hard enough now. When there's a noise in the house — when the dogs throw up, who wakes up? I do.

BOB: *(Chuckles to himself.)* It took me many nights to master this. I just lie perfectly still and act as though I'm in deep sleep mode — like this . . . *(Asleep beside her, he begins to snore.)*

LISA: I lay there yelling for him — "BOB! *(No answer.)* BOB!" *(No answer.)*

BOB: One more time and she'll get up.

LISA: BOB! And there you have it — I get up. And — OUCH! I trip over his shoes that he kicks in the middle of the room.

BOB: Every night I place my shoes in the same place, but she manages to trip over them.

LISA: The only reason he'd get up is if *he* smells smoke — and that's to save himself.

BOB: Smells — I hate smells. Liver, spoiled milk, Reuben casserole, and now we can add dirty diapers to the list. Don't look at me to change the diapers.

LISA: He thinks he'll never change a diaper.

BOB: I'll hand the baby to her — then act as though the baby just did it. See? Here's my surprise look. *(Puts his hand on his face — looking surprised.)*

LISA: It's normal — in one end out the other.

BOB: Oh — and the spit-up. I have such a weak stomach.

LISA: Then there's spit-up. He has no stomach.

BOB: If it spits up, I'll spit up.

LISA: If the baby spits up, he'll follow. It'll be like two kids.

BOB: Kids. One leads to two and two leads to three and after that? Oh, no, from now on, I'll withhold sex.

LISA: God, he's thinking of more kids. Oh, no! The hell if we have sex again!

BOB: She's giving me the "we're not having sex anymore" look.

LISA: He has no idea how sensitive I am at this moment.

BOB: What the hell's her problem?

LISA: I can see my future — a mom, grandmother, great grandmother, a rest home — last, the funeral home.

BOB: God, she's going to be just like her mother. *(He does the cuckoo sign.)* The cycle begins.

LISA: I hope it's *not* a boy.

BOB: I hope it *is* a boy.

LISA: Two Bobs are enough. I mean — Robert Rob Roberts the third.

BOB: All my life, I thought if I have a son, I'd carry on the name. It's about pride — my father.

LISA: It's all about him. It'll be a headache. Holidays — you say "Bob" and you'll have three of them staring at you. I hope it's a girl.

BOB: I hope it's not a girl. I know *nothing* about girls — especially when their bodies go through "the change." I have no understanding of that — from a parent's perspective.

LISA: We'll get in constant mother-daughter arguments.

BOB: She'll never date that's for sure. I know what boys are thinking. That's how I got in this mess.

LISA: *(Acts as though she's disciplining a child.)* Discipline — yes. No. Yes! No! No! No! NO! YES! NO! THAT'S IT, YOU'RE GROUNDED!

BOB: *(Acts as though he's disciplining the same child.)* IF YOU DO THAT, YOU GOT ANOTHER THING COMING!

LISA: I'M VERY DISAPPOINTED IN YOU! WHAT WERE YOU THINKING!

BOB: WHAT DID I TELL YOU? WHAT DID I TELL YOU?

LISA: *(Gasp.)* I am my mother.

BOB: *(Gasp.)* I am my father. Oh no —

LISA AND BOB: *(Realization.)* Evolution.

BOB: Questions —

LISA: They'll ask me things that don't pertain to buying a home.

BOB: *(Imitates a child.)* "Why is the sky blue?"

LISA: *(Also imitates a child.)* "Why is your hair gray?"

BOB: "Can I have a raise in my allowance?"

LISA: "Where do babies come from?"

BOB: "What's a penis?"

LISA: "Do I have one?"

BOB: "How come no one likes your music?"

LISA: "How come no one buys houses from you?"

BOB: *(Beat.)* "What's bestiality?"

LISA: Is this it? Will I *ever* sell another home?

BOB: Will I *ever* write another song?

LISA: Will I ever be able to relax again?

BOB: Will I ever have sex again?

LISA: Unbelievable, he's thinking about sex. Again!

BOB: Will I?

LISA: This is the biggest commitment I've ever faced.

BOB: I'm a loner — having a wife was a moment of weakness.

LISA: My career will be ruined!

BOB: Light! I have to find the light for my piano!

LISA: I can't do this!

BOB: Absolutely not!

LISA: Unworkable!

BOB: Impossible!

LISA: Unfeasible!

BOB: Impracticable!

LISA: This is too much.

BOB: *Way* too much.

LISA AND BOB: NO!

(They snap back to the exact position they were in before their consciences started speaking. They look at each other nervously.)

LISA: *(To Bob.)* Sure you're ready?

BOB: *(To Lisa.)* Of course. You?

LISA: Absolutely. Let's look together.

BOB: Wait —

LISA: You don't, do you?

BOB: No — the symbols. I need to know —

LISA: A circle with the line through it means we are.

BOB: Got it.

LISA: Ready?

BOB: Ready.

(He takes his hanky and picks up the pregnancy test. They hold hands as he raises the results up so they both can see.)

That's a line through it — that means —

(Beat.)

LISA: You're a daddy.

BOB: And you're a mommy.

(Silence. Smile.)

LISA: Oh, Bob.

BOB: Oh, Lisa

BOB AND LISA: *(They kiss. Beat. Stop and look out to the audience. Their consciences speak to the audience.)* Oh, no.

(Blackout.)

END OF PLAY

The Same Thing

LISA SOLAND

The Same Thing was first produced by TeCo Theatrical
Productions, Inc. as part of their 2005 New Play Competition
in Dallas, Texas. Lisa Soland directed the play, Rachel Lamb
choreographed, Carter Hudson played Man and
Danni Wilkins played Woman.

CHARACTERS
>WOMAN: a woman, any age
>MAN: a man, any age

SETTING
>The aisle of a grocery store

TIME
>Now

• • •

At Rise: Man enters stage left and Woman stage right, pushing shopping carts partially filled with food and beverages. She is shopping facing downstage and he is shopping facing upstage. As they come near to each other, instead of one going one way and the other going the other way, they run into each other. In hopes to remedy the situation, they each move to get out of the way, once again . . . running into each other. Believe it or not, they do this one more time and then begin to laugh.

WOMAN: *(Laughing.)* Care for a dance?
>*(Continuing to laugh, they both get out of the way and begin to cross by each other and away.)*
MAN: I'm so sorry.
WOMAN: It's my fault, really.
MAN: Oh, I'd hardly say it was your fault. We both just seem to be thinking along the same lines.
WOMAN: Yes, we are aren't we?
MAN: Yes, it's interesting.
WOMAN: How so?
MAN: Well . . . never mind.
>*(He continues to exit stage right.)*
WOMAN: No, really. I'd like to hear.
MAN: *(He stops to explain.)* Well, if one of us were not as kind, more rude I should say, we wouldn't be having this problem at all.
WOMAN: We're running into each other because we're kind?
MAN: Yes. See, we're courteous people. We are of the like that try to accommodate the environmental space of another.

WOMAN: *(Nodding.)* Yes, I see what you're saying.

MAN: Therefore, we both try at the same time to move out of the way, resulting only in . . .

WOMAN: . . . getting back into the way of the other.

MAN: Yes. Very exciting, actually.

WOMAN: Exciting?

MAN: Oh, yes. You see, in all my past relationships, I've always been "the adjustor," the one who gets out of the way, the one who apologizes when it's needed so that the relationship can continue. I've never really had the thought to actively pursue one who is more like me — kind.

WOMAN: That *is* interesting. I have a similar background. My past relationships have been nothing but struggle. Trying hard, very hard to please and then waking up one day and realizing that I'm the only one who's trying. "The lone and selfless giver." That's me.

MAN: You got it, exactly. This is quite amazing. I've never really run into another . . . me.

WOMAN: Well, I'm sure we're different in other ways.

MAN: Really? You think so?

WOMAN: Oh, we must be. Everyone's different, aren't they?

MAN: Well, let's see.

(He turns his shopping cart around and faces her.)

Do you like to tango?

WOMAN: Actually, I do. I happen to love it. I've studied since I was five.

MAN: Five?

WOMAN: Yes.

MAN: Me too.

WOMAN: No kidding.

MAN: Five. I kid you not. I love it passionately.

WOMAN: Oh, that's just a coincidence. Remarkable, at that.

MAN: Yes, I'd say so.

WOMAN: *(She turns her cart around and faces him.)* How many brothers and sisters do you have?

MAN: Three.

WOMAN: Me too.

MAN: Two brothers and one sister.

WOMAN: Me too, exactly. Where do you fall?

MAN: I'm third.

WOMAN: Me too.

MAN: Third?

WOMAN: Yes.

MAN: Remarkable.

WOMAN: This is getting quite hard to believe.

MAN: Oh, I don't know. It was bound to happen at some point. You spend a lifetime running into people who are different from you . . .

WOMAN: Very different.

MAN: Yes.

WOMAN: *(With some pain.)* Different and difficult.

MAN: Yes, very different and then suddenly one day, presto — a match.

WOMAN: *(Tentatively.)* Well, I don't know if I'd say we were a match.

MAN: *(Recognizing her tentativeness.)* Oh, very sorry. I was not insinuating that we . . . the two of us . . .

WOMAN: . . . get together?

MAN: No, not at all. I'm single but I would never presume that you were.

WOMAN: I am, actually.

MAN: Single?

WOMAN: Yes.

(Beat.)

Very.

MAN: What do you know about that?

WOMAN: But still . . .

MAN: Oh, yes. But still we can't just assume that we, the two of us, would ever . . . go out.

WOMAN: Well, if we did . . . go out . . .

MAN: Yes?

WOMAN: If we did, I'm sure we would find, through continued conversation, many areas where we differ.

MAN: Of course, it's natural.

WOMAN: What we're experiencing now, is *not* natural.

MAN: Not based on my experience.

WOMAN: *(She steps toward him quickly and asks . . .)* Do you go to church?

MAN: *(Stepping toward her quickly.)* Every Sunday.

WOMAN: You're kidding? I thought for sure I'd get you there.

MAN: Nope, every Sunday.

(Quickly turning out to audience.)

Early service?

WOMAN: *(Turns out as well.)* Every time. Starts the day out right.

MAN: You are a woman after my own heart.

WOMAN: You know, this is remarkable. To be quite honest, I've always wanted to marry a man who already went to church, you know?

MAN: Yes. So you wouldn't have to talk him into it.

WOMAN: Exactly. I tried that.

MAN: Didn't work, huh?

WOMAN: Well, it does, you know. For a while. Then when they've got you, here . . .

(She points to her heart.)

. . . in the heart . . . it fades. It all fades.

MAN: *(Nodding.)* Yes. I've dated many fading women.

WOMAN: I guess the trick is to marry someone you like as they are, right from the start.

MAN: Yes, the problem is finding someone you like.

WOMAN: Yes.

MAN: I suppose it would be narcissistic of us if we were to . . . go out.

WOMAN: Narcissistic? Why?

MAN: Well, it would be like dating ourselves. Like the ol' clown falling in love with his reflection. I'm sure it would fail, eventually. We would have nothing to talk about.

WOMAN: We don't seem to be having a problem yet.

MAN: Yes, that's true. But still, I suppose one needs conflict in their lives, for . . . *(Trying to think.)* . . . something, right?

WOMAN: Conflict?

MAN: Yes, you know. To keep you on your toes.

(He stands on his toes to demonstrate.)

WOMAN: I'm tired of being on my toes. I'd actually like to be able to stand using all parts of my feet.

MAN: Yes. That does sound appealing, doesn't it?

(They share a moment of depth and intimacy that he breaks by glancing into her shopping cart.)

MAN: *(Continued.)* Oh, I see you like frozen dinners as well.

(He takes one of his "Hungry Man" frozen dinners out of his cart.)

WOMAN: Well, I don't actually like them.

(She takes one of her "Healthy Choice" frozen dinners out of her cart.)

I buy them because I don't like to cook.

MAN: *(Excited, he steps toward her.)* Oh, you don't like to cook? I love to cook.

WOMAN: *(Clarifying.)* Well . . . I don't like to cook for just me.

MAN: Yes, it's horrible. That's why *I* buy the testy things.

(He tosses his dinner back into his cart.)

WOMAN: Yes, they're great. Just pop them into the oven and wah-lah.

MAN: Yes, very convenient.

(Quickly.)

Do you like to give or receive?

WOMAN: Pardon?

MAN: *(More gently.)* Do you like to give or receive?

WOMAN: *(It occurs to her what he's saying and is embarrassed.)* Oh . . . my.

MAN: I'm sorry to embarrass you but I've got to know, it's killing me.

WOMAN: Oh.

MAN: Actually, I probably already know the answer — give, right?

WOMAN: *(Sweetly.)* Well . . . yes.

MAN: Me too. And there lies our healthy conflict.

WOMAN: Excuse me?

MAN: Our healthy conflict. We would both have to learn to receive. Look . . .

> *(Beat.)*

> What's your name?

WOMAN: Jean.

MAN: Jean?! No way!! No WAY!!!

WOMAN: Yes, my name is Jean.

MAN: *My* name is Gene.

WOMAN: Oh, my God.

MAN: I can't believe it. This is the Twilight Zone, right here and now.

WOMAN: I feel like I'm dreaming.

MAN: Man, if this is a dream, let us sleep on! This is remarkable. The most remarkable day of my life!!!

WOMAN: *(Trying to remain composed.)* Well, now. Let's keep our heads. You were saying?

MAN: *(Due to her hesitancy, also trying to remain composed.)* Yes, Jean . . . not that you and I are going to . . .

WOMAN: Date.

MAN: Date, yes. I don't want to presume that we would conclude this conversation in dating, but if we were . . .

WOMAN: If.

MAN: If we were . . . to go out . . .

> *(They both move slowly toward each other during the next few lines.)*

MAN: *(Continued.)* . . . since we are by nature, givers, we would have to then learn to receive.

> *(They move closer.)*

WOMAN: Therefore, living a much more balanced . . .

MAN: . . . and fulfilling . . .

> *(Closer.)*

WOMAN: Existence.

MAN: Exactly.

> *(They go to . . . maybe kiss, then she pulls away.)*

WOMAN: It's too much really.

MAN: Too much?

WOMAN: Yes. It's almost too much to handle.

(She hides behind her cart and without knowing, steps up on the back bar.)
We're finishing each other's sentences!

MAN: *(Growing nervous, he crosses to the front of her cart.)* So, what are you saying?

(When she answers, he listens so intently, that without knowing he pushes her around upstage, in half a circle, during the next few lines.)

WOMAN: I'm not used to this . . . this functioning communication and it's hard for me.

MAN: If being happy and fulfilled is hard for you . . .

WOMAN: If you only knew what I've been through . . .

MAN: . . . and it would be cause for you to walk away . . .

WOMAN: . . . the experiences I've had over and over and over again.

MAN: . . . then there's where we differ.

WOMAN: We differ?

(The cart movement stops.)

MAN: Yes. Because I would never walk away from anything that had a pinch of a promise that by moving forward, I would be more happy. Never.

WOMAN: Yes, that is where we differ.

(She steps down off bar on back of cart.)
New things are very hard for me.

MAN: The tango was new for you, at one time.

WOMAN: I was five.

MAN: *(To move closer, he steps up on front of cart.)* You can be five again.

(Woman is hesitating so he takes her by the hands and kneels down on one knee in front of her.)

MAN: *(Continued.)* Look, Jean. I would like to date you, to take you out on the town, to wine and dine you with fabulous homemade meals and treat you . . . well, to give and give and give to you, but I understand completely, if because of fear, you have to say no.

WOMAN: *(Moving away.)* No.

(Beat.)
It's not for me, Gene. I'm very sorry.

MAN: *(Sadly defeated, he rises and dusts off pants.)* I understand. It's all right. Well, good-bye, Jean.

(He steps in to shake her hand.)

WOMAN: *(Shaking his hand.)* Good-bye . . . Gene.

MAN: *(Deeply sincere.)* It's been more than a pleasure talking with you.

WOMAN: *(Deeply sincere.)* Same to you.

(They cross back to their carts and start to go but both try to go the same way again. They smile kindly, and then both try to get out of each other's way by going in the same direction . . . again. Believe it or not, it happens a third time and then they stop.)

WOMAN: *(Continued.) (Recognizing that this is a sign, she gives in.)* Well, what do you know about that? We're doing the same thing.

MAN: The same thing. What do you know.

(Having already moved on, he tries to exit.)

WOMAN: *(Coyly, she steps in his path, stopping him.)* I don't mind the same thing . . . Gene.

MAN: *(Hopeful.)* The same thing is good.

WOMAN: *(She takes a single rose out of her cart.)* Care for a tango?

MAN: *(He pushes his cart out of the way.)* I thought you'd never ask.

(The tango music begins and they quickly snap into the starting position. She puts the rose between her teeth and they begin. She leads and the two dance stage right and then he leads and the two dance stage left. On their way off-stage she turns and swoops up her purse and off they go with flare. Music swells.)

(Blackout.)

END OF PLAY

An Honest Arrangement

DAVID WIENER

An Honest Arrangement was first produced at the Lyceum
Theatre in San Diego, California. It was directed by Lia Metz
and starred Karina Montgomery as Nara and David Rethoret as
Willie. It won Best Play in the 12th Annual New York City
Fifteen Minute Play Festival, presented by Turnip Theatre
Company in association with American Globe Theatre
(April 2006). The New York production was directed by Ivan
Magrin-Chagnolleau and starred Joan Fishman as Nara and
Stan Tracy as Willie.

CHARACTERS

WILLIE: anywhere from sixty to seventy years old. A retired, generally optimistic guy with a gaping hole in his life caused by the death of his wife.

NARA: early 30s; she's had it tough and is hoping to find a way out of a pretty miserable existence.

SETTING

A large airport in America (a row of folding chairs will do just fine)

TIME

Present

• • •

An empty stage, except for a row of folding chairs.

At Rise: Before the lights come up, we hear the sounds of a major international airport: People talking, luggage carts moving along, some muddled flight announcements. The lights come up, revealing a Man in late middle age (well, very late middle age, truth to tell) sitting nervously on one of the folding chairs. Although is nicely turned out, he is wilted. He tugs at his tie, something he isn't used to wearing. There is a bouquet of flowers on his lap. We hear an announcement over the speaker system.

AIRPORT ANNOUNCER'S VOICE: Passengers now arriving on flight 412 from New York, Gate 26-B. Thank you for your patience and, again, our apologies for the delay.

(The Man gets up slowly; he is stiff and sore. He nervously finger-combs his hair and pulls a photo out of his jacket pocket. He watches the arriving passengers as they walk past him, comparing them to the photo. Of course, he's the only one who sees these passengers, since this is a two-person playlet. A Woman at least twenty years younger than the Man enters, limping and cradling a ratty carry-on bag. She is also holding a photo. They see each other, take another look at the photos, then turn the photos toward each other.)

MAN: *(Gesturing with the photo.)* Nara? Are you Nara?

NARA: *(Gesturing with the photo she has.)* Yes, yes. Nara, me. You are Willie?

WILLIE: Yes! That's me. Boy, I was beginning to think you'd never get here!

NARA: Yes, I have been in three different airplanes to get all the way to here. And a delay from New York of two hours.

WILLIE: Well, you must be just about beat.

(Willie does some juggling with the flowers. First, he holds them between his knees and reaches out for Nara's bag. Just as she holds the bag out, Willie realizes he shouldn't hold his fiancée's flowers between his legs and grabs the flowers, resulting in Nara's bag hitting the floor.)

WILLIE: *(Continued.)* *(Picking up the bag and thrusting the flowers into Nara's hands.)* Oops — sorry, sorry, sorry — here, there we are . . .

NARA: Thanks you. They are quite pretty.

WILLIE: I just want to say, welcome to America and hello, it is *so* nice to finally —

NARA: *(Looking again at the photo of Willie.)* Exact.

WILLIE: Sorry?

NARA: *(Disappointed.)* Your photo. Is exact. You are exact like picture.

WILLIE: You sound kind of disappointed.

NARA: Exact like picture.

WILLIE: Well, I didn't want to mislead you or anything. Some guys use Photoshop to make their picture look, you know, kinda better — younger? With their computer? And I wanted to make sure you knew just what you were getting. Honesty's the best policy. Right?

NARA: Yes. Honest is best. We get married now?

WILLIE: Uh, well, not right this minute. That'll be tomorrow morning at the County Clerk's office.

NARA: I am here for that; I am not a concubine. The arrangement is marriage. An honest arrangement was made.

WILLIE: Oh, absolutely! It's all set for tomorrow, all legal and honest. Umn –
(Flustered and kind of overwhelmed.)
Here, let's — let's just — have a seat for a minute . . .
(Willie takes Nara over to the row of chairs and helps her sit. She takes her bag and pulls out a dictionary/phrasebook.)

NARA: I have been fully honest with you at all times.

WILLIE: Yes, and I appreciate it.

NARA: *(Tapping her leg; it's artificial.)* Honest about everything. That I am without a limb from unrest.

WILLIE: Yes, I understand completely and I appreciated your telling me in your very first e-mail —

NARA: I was studying for nurse.
(Points to the front of her artificial leg, then to the back of her artificial leg.)
Entrance, exit, through and through. Bone and artery, then removed. There is no option with so much serious wound.

WILLIE: No.

NARA: Men in Azerbaijan find it . . .

(Pauses, trying to think of the word, then flips through her dictionary.)
. . . Ah!

(Slaps the dictionary shut, triumphant that she found the right word.)
"Revolting"!

WILLIE: Oh . . . well, that's not right. It's not revolting.

NARA: When we marry, I will continue my studies here for nurse. You will not
be so miserable lonely, I will finish my school and work part-time and
also look after you since you are already old man.

WILLIE: Oh, well, that's real nice, thank you so much . . .

NARA: This is all honest truth, correct? To our arrangement? We are both not
children. I have already more than thirty years. I get to escape unrest and
you get new wife to look after you.

WILLIE: Well, I suppose so, but that's putting it in rather unemotional terms.

NARA: I think we both cannot afford emotion. Your wife is dead and your
grown-up child lives far away. As you e-mailed?

WILLIE: Yes, just like I said.

NARA: And I am dropout unmarried nurse student, which no sane man back
home would touch and I have one leg already rotted in the grave.

WILLIE: *(Pause.)* Hey, what do you say we stop at the bar? They have a real nice
bar at this airport and I could sure use a drink right now and I'll sure bet
you could sure use —

NARA: — It is better that we drink at the wedding.

WILLIE: *(Desperate for a drink.)* Oh! OK.

NARA: So everything is good, correct?

WILLIE: Oh, certainly! Everything is — working out — just fine.

NARA: Your daughter is informed about her father's new wife?

WILLIE: Yes. She is informed.

NARA: I am betting that she is very angry.

WILLIE: Well, "unhappy" would be a better way of putting it.

NARA: Of course. Mother is dead and father marries some woman on Internet. And she fears to lose any inheritance.

WILLIE: Ah, yes, she did raise some concerns along those lines.

NARA: If your daughter was here living with you and looking after you, you
would not have made this arrangement with someone like me.

WILLIE: Oh, well, I —

NARA: Honest, please. Honest.

WILLIE: I — no, probably not, I guess. But she's got a family of her own and
they live 2,000 miles away and, well . . .

NARA: Of course. I understand. It is the situation and we all make the best.
Of course she will hate me.

WILLIE: She'll get used to the idea.

NARA: No, she will not. I would not if I were her. But she will make the best.

WILLIE: I suppose so.

(Pause.)

NARA: I go to church. Each week, always.

WILLIE: Yes! You said. That's beautiful. Faith is great.

NARA: You will help me find a church near your house?

WILLIE: Already taken care of. There is a Russian Orthodox church about twelve miles away. I got the directions. We can check it out any time you like.

NARA: Thank you. Very important to me that I have my church.

WILLIE: I understand.

NARA: When I was a girl with two legs, I would always go to my church and sit in the same place every time.

WILLIE: That sounds very comforting.

NARA: I would sit in that same place because I always saw a miracle. Have you ever seen a miracle?

WILLIE: At my age, every day with a working prostate pretty much counts as a miracle. But, no I'd have to say I've never actually seen one. You did, huh?

NARA: I did, yes. Every week. Some people, they laugh at such things and don't want to hear. I will keep silent about this if you prefer.

WILLIE: Not me! I like miracles. It's just that they're the kind of things that always seem to happen to somebody else.

NARA: I will tell you about mine, then. Since I was a little girl, each week, a miraculous vision would appear to me. I sat in the church and I would watch the stained-glass window. In this window were placed small cut-glass jewels of glass with no color at all. And the sun would move as we prayed God and, eventually, the sun would find these cut-glass jewels. And then — the white light of the sun would turn wonderfully into every color God wants us to see. A rainbow. It made me catch my breath.

WILLIE: — then what happened?

NARA: That *is* what happened.

WILLIE: That's the miracle.

NARA: Yes!

WILLIE: Oh.

NARA: (Laughs.) You think I am ignorant. No. I am a cultured woman, I am educated at university. I also have science classes when a schoolchild. The complete spectrum of light, as whiteness, enters the glass jewel. This acts as a prism to separate — "refract," I learned the English — the light into all constituent frequencies. And there is the rainbow. Explained first by Newton, Isaac, an Englishman.

WILLIE: So — you know it's just optics? No miracle?

NARA: It *is* a miracle! Each time it happens. You see? Optics is the miracle!

WILLIE: But — you just said — Newton explained it.

NARA: Yes, Newton *explains* it. But Newton does not *make* it.

WILLIE: Oh.

(Pause.)

Well, I suppose you could look at it that way. So — should we go pick up your luggage?

NARA: *(Picks up her bag.)* All done.

WILLIE: Just your carry-on? You didn't check any suitcases through?

NARA: No. This is everything. Nothing else worth taking. As I told you. No family, my parents are dead and I have had no husband. As I e-mailed, there is no one back there for me. No one back there. What kind of car do you have?

WILLIE: Uh — it's a Honda. About six years old.

NARA: *(Pulls a document out of her bag.)* I have obtained an international driver's license. But you must teach me how to drive on freeways so we will not be killed to death. I learn quickly. I am an educated woman.

WILLIE: Yes. I remember, you went to college.

NARA: And then, once I am trained to drive properly, I can be the one who drives you as you continue to become even older.

WILLIE: Gosh. That — sounds like a great plan . . .

NARA: I am already almost a nurse. I know how the body will decay. But we make the best. You will be able to go places because I will drive you when after you teach me. You need not fear —

(Consults her dictionary.)

"housebound."

WILLIE: Well, this is a cheery conversation. Let's just leave all that for the moment, since I can still manage to pull on my own pants —

NARA: You will be able to get to your many, many doctors' appointments because I will take you. And to go play checkers with your other very old friends who are not yet died. Is there room in the car to hold medical equipment?

WILLIE: *What* medical equipment?!

NARA: Your wheelchair. Your oxygen tank.

WILLIE: I don't have any of that stuff! There's nothing in my trunk but fishing gear and a six-pack! Look, I gotta tell you, I ran a 5K last summer! That's like a *marathon* for someone my age, OK?

NARA: For the future. If this equipment is needed. There is room in your car?

WILLIE: *(Sighs.)* Yes. Sure, I suppose so. But let's not rush things, OK?

NARA: To be prepared is good.

> *(Pause.)*
>
> To make the best.

WILLIE: Yeah, sure. But —

NARA: That is why you are finding me and e-mailing me and exchanging pictures and now marrying me. To be prepared, correct? Honest, please.

WILLIE: Well, that's a part of it, I guess a fair part of it, but there's more to life than just, you know, looking ahead to falling apart. We can have fun in the meantime; get out, do things. You — you wrote that you liked movies, I remember.

NARA: Yes, I enjoy cinema very much. Very. My uncle was film director back home.

WILLIE: Really?

NARA: Yes, he made several films. But they were too political and police agents put a bomb and his car blows up to pieces. But he is not killed, he has to —
> *(Consults the dictionary.)*

— "flee." Now he makes the pornography in Germany. I am honest, so I tell you this.

WILLIE: No kidding?

NARA: If he goes home, I think they kill him right this time. So he stays in Germany.

WILLIE: *(Picks up Nara's bag.)* Well, an uncle in the arts, gee, that's nice. I tell you what. Let's head out to the car and we'll go to a restaurant with a pretty view and —
> *(Nara is crying and she's suddenly getting very upset.)*

WILLIE: What is it? What's wrong? *I* don't mind about your uncle, for God's sake! Is that what you're crying about? What is it?

NARA: *(Almost wailing.)* Oh, Willie! I am . . . *not* honest. Oh, Willie . . .

WILLIE: *(Sits down and puts his hand on her shoulder.)* About what? What is it?

NARA: I am *not* honest, I am a liar.

WILLIE: What do you mean? Lying about what?

NARA: *(Crying.)* Oh, Willie, I said there was no one back there for me. A big lie. There *is* someone back there! Willie, I am sorry.

WILLIE: What, you — have a husband or something?

NARA: Oh, Willie. I am not honest. I have my *daughter* back there.

WILLIE: You never said anything about a daughter.

NARA: Of course not! My daughter was with a man I was not married to. Ten years ago. Before my leg. I put her to live with my aunt to come here. To come here where I can make more money than anywhere else so I can send some to her. So I lied, I was not honest.

WILLIE: Why didn't you just *say* you had a daughter?

NARA: Oh, Willie. Look at me. Look! Over thirty. A whole leg gone? *And* a daughter to support? With all those other girls, so younger and prettier with no children and two good and sexy legs! *I* compete with them for American men who want to marry a foreign girl?! I am sorry, Willie. I am a liar. Now, I am honest. There.

(Pause.)

I will do what you want, you decide. But now I am at some peace with myself.

WILLIE: Well. Look. It's — OK, it'll be OK. It's just — the situation. Right?

NARA: *(Sniffling, wiping her eyes.)* Yes.

WILLIE: And in — the situation — we make the best. Right?

NARA: Willie. The agreement was broken by my end because I lied.

WILLIE: I think — it's OK. We make the best — see?

(Nara nods quickly, still sniffling. She looks up at him.)

NARA: Willie. I am — a little frightened, I think.

(Willie helps her up.)

WILLIE: We'll be OK, you'll see. First, we'll get something good to eat. And I'll drive us past that church on the way home. Would you like that? Would you like to take a look at that church?

NARA: Yes, Willie. I would — like that very.

WILLIE: Then that's what we'll do. We'll go there — and we'll go inside — and find a quiet place to sit. And, if we look around — I bet we'll even see a rainbow . . .

(Willie walks Nara out of the airport, as the lights fade to black.)

END OF PLAY

PLAYS FOR
TWO
WOMEN

Bone China

K. Alexa Mavromatis

Bone China was a semifinalist in the 12th Annual New York City Fifteen Minute Play Festival, presented by Turnip Theatre Company and American Globe Theatre, April 2006. The production was directed by the author, and the cast was as follows: Lainie — D'Arcy Dersham; Mary — Rachel Carney. The stage directions and other notes included here were created for that production. *Bone China* was also included in Boston Theatre Marathon VIII, presented by Boston Playwrights' Theatre and produced by Actors' Shakespeare Project, May 2006.

CHARACTERS

MARY: twenty-seven

LAINIE: Mary's sister, twenty-nine

SETTING

The attic of Mary and Lainie's childhood home, filled with boxes, random items on shelves, old furniture, clothing racks, etc.

TIME

Saturday, mid-afternoon

• • •

As the lights come up, we see Mary upstage center, standing in the doorway of the attic. She is watching Lainie, who sits upstage center right, surrounded by boxes of random items from storage and assorted remnants of their childhood: Barbie dolls, stuffed animals, Sassy *magazines, popsicle-stick art projects, neckties, paperback books, etc. Lainie is repeatedly tapping a Magic Eight Ball on the floor to remove the bubbles from the ball, and flipping it over to "answer" her questions. Lainie wears a scarf on her head.*

MARY: What are you doing?

LAINIE: Just going through all this freaky stuff.

MARY: *(Crossing to Lainie, then kneeling.)* What's that?

LAINIE: *(Holding up a misshapen furry lump.)* I think it was a stuffed animal . . . once.

MARY: I don't remember him.

LAINIE: Well, he was either mine or yours.

MARY: What is . . . *was* he?

LAINIE: I have no idea, poor thing.

MARY: Why would Mom hang on to that?

LAINIE: Mom kept everything — c'mon. Put him over there. That's the "go" pile.

MARY: *(Throwing the animal on the pile, downstage center left.)* You don't have to do this.

LAINIE: I know.

(Handing Mary a small china teacup — the kind from a child's play set — from a box.)

Do you remember these?

MARY: Oh yeah. It says "Bone China" on here . . . Isn't that really good?

LAINIE: It's the strongest . . .

MARY: *(Digging through box.)* That's kind of fancy for little kids . . .

LAINIE: That was Mom.

MARY: There aren't any more cups in here. But here's the sugar . . .

LAINIE: *Someone* broke them.

MARY: Me? No!

LAINIE: Yes.

MARY: I did not.

LAINIE: *(Placing cup on top of an unopened box, center.)* And now this one's the sole survivor.

MARY: How many were there?

LAINIE: Like six or something.

MARY: There were not.

LAINIE: Yes . . .

MARY: Really?

LAINIE: *(Crossing downstage right to small stack of boxes, and grabbing another box to sort.)* I remember when Laurie Jennings was over one time you kept running into my room and grabbing them one by one and running away. I thought you were hiding them.

MARY: I do *not* remember that.

LAINIE: You were probably throwing them off the roof or something.

MARY: OK, enough. Are you going to be up here the whole weekend?

LAINIE: I dunno.

MARY: You shouldn't spend your whole weekend this way.

LAINIE: It's kind of fun. It kind of gives you a snapshot of Mom's head.

MARY: Scary place.

LAINIE: Mary . . .

MARY: I know. I'm kidding. You know I loved Mom.

LAINIE: I know.

(Slight pause.)

MARY: I can't believe that was two years ago.

LAINIE: Yeah. I'm really glad you've been able to be here with Dad.

MARY: Me too.

LAINIE: I mean it. He's glad you're here. It's been hard for him.

MARY: I know.

LAINIE: I can't help but feel a little bad . . .

MARY: Why?

LAINIE: You haven't had a chance to lead your own life. I got sick right after
you graduated college. Then Mom. Now . . .

MARY: I don't even want to talk about this, Lainie, really . . .

LAINIE: But I worry about you.

MARY: *(Standing.)* Do you want to go for a walk or something?

LAINIE: No, I'm good.

MARY: A movie?

LAINIE: Seriously, Mary, I'm having a good time . . . It's fine.

MARY: I just . . .

LAINIE: You should help me.

MARY: I don't think . . .

LAINIE: I know — you don't think I should waste a weekend this way.

MARY: No, I don't.

LAINIE: Especially now that my weekends are numbered.

MARY: Lainie!

LAINIE: I know you were thinking that. What if I want to spend my weekend
going through stuff in the attic? Because I'm glad to have a chance to do
it?

MARY: OK, OK.

LAINIE: You should help me . . .

MARY: OK.

LAINIE: . . . and stop giving me a hard time.

MARY: OK.

LAINIE: I'm fine.

MARY: Alright. Jeez. Have you seen my blue coat up here?
(Crosses upstage to the door, and shuts it to look behind it.)
The last time I saw it, it was behind . . .

LAINIE: *(Jumping up.)* Wait!

MARY: What?

LAINIE: Can you open the door?

MARY: *(Frozen.)* Oh shit!

LAINIE: That's why we always leave this door open.

MARY: I know — fuck, I forgot.

LAINIE: Can you open the door?

MARY: *(Trying to open the door.)* No.

LAINIE: We'll have to wait until Dad gets home, then — unless the screwdriver's still on top of the molding . . .
(Mary feels the frame above the door.)

MARY: Nope.

LAINIE: Crap.

MARY: Sorry. I remember that day Dad got shut up here and had to wait for us to get back from shopping. Now.

LAINIE: It's OK.

(Mary crosses right to a small pile of items Lainie has sorted and has decided to keep. Lainie surveys the room and crosses to a small sofa covered by a sheet, left. She sits and takes a few items out of a box that has been sitting on the sofa — a book, a toy rocket, a purse. Lost in thought, she mumbles something.)

MARY: What?

LAINIE: Nothing.

MARY: What were you going to say?

LAINIE: Just going through all this stuff . . . I was thinking I'm glad Mom's dead.

MARY: Lainie!

LAINIE: No, I mean, I'm not actually glad Mom is dead — you know that. I'm just . . . I'm just glad she didn't have to see me go through surgery this time.

MARY: Yeah.

LAINIE: I remember, one time at the hospital . . .

(Shifting to sit on the arm of the sofa.)

I just think it's hard for parents to watch their kids go through stuff like that. Especially since the prognosis isn't, uh, so good now . . . Of course, that means Sarah won't grow up knowing her mother *or* her grandmother.

MARY: *(Crossing to Lainie and sitting on a small stool right of the sofa.)* But she'll have Nathan, and Dad . . .

LAINIE: And you.

MARY: Yeah.

LAINIE: It's weird. I mean we lost Mom, and we didn't plan for it. We *couldn't* plan for it — a drunk guy crossed over the center line and that was it. Now, we get to plan. I get to think about places I want to go to, people I want to see . . . stuff that's supposed to be fun to think about. Do you know what I mean? It's fucked up.

MARY: Do you know what you're going to tell Sarah?

LAINIE: She's too young, really. To understand. That's something Nathan's going to have to deal with later.

MARY: He'll do great.

LAINIE: I know. He's an amazing dad. Listen, just don't ever tell Sarah "Your Mommy went to sleep" or anything weird like that, OK? You're not supposed to do that.

MARY: I won't.

LAINIE: It'll mess her up — she'll need a night-light until she's twenty-five or something. Tell her . . . just tell her that mommy went to heaven and is looking out for her or something . . . But don't say I'm *watching* her — that sounds creepy.

(Slight pause.)

MARY: Do you believe in heaven?

LAINIE: I dunno. You know, to tell you the truth: I'm twenty-nine years old, I'm leaving a husband I thought I'd get old with, a two-year-old daughter . . . Heaven is about the last thing I want to spend time thinking about now.

MARY: Yeah.

LAINIE: In fact, it kind of makes me mad that it's what I'm *expected* to think about now.

(Pause, as Lainie crosses downstage right to boxes, pulls out a poster and throws it on the "go" pile. She continues to look through the box, distracted.)

She won't remember me, you know.

MARY: Don't say that! Of course . . .

LAINIE: No, she won't. And I'm not trying to be humble or melodramatic or whatever. I read this big thing about it online. The average age of your first memory is three-and-a-half.

MARY: Really?

LAINIE: What's your first memory?

MARY: *(Shifting from the stool to the sofa.)* Grandpa Jack's funeral.

LAINIE: See? I was six, so you were four-ish.

MARY: What's yours?

LAINIE: I was trying to think of that when I was reading. It's not a memory, exactly . . . well, it is, but it's not a specific event or anything. I think the first thing I remember is standing outside in the backyard, with the tulips. I remember thinking they were really tall.

(Slight pause.)

Anyway, it was this whole study . . . It's a lack of autobiographical memory. At that age. Sometimes, very young children will remember major life events — like Grandpa Jack's funeral — but some best-case scenario for a first memory of your mom, huh?

MARY: You just have to make every day a major life event.

LAINIE: *(Laughing slightly.)* Yeah, no pressure. You're such an optimist. You want to hear something funny?

MARY: What?

LAINIE: My tumor — the one with the long-ass name I still can't pronounce right — can take three to five years to grow to the size it was when they removed it. That means I had it when I was pregnant with Sarah. I was growing life and death at the same time. Crazy, huh?

MARY: Yeah. Crazy.

LAINIE: I've been thinking too much. They should have taken out my entire brain. No more reading, though. I was telling Nathan the other day I'm declaring a moratorium on research. *That's* what wears you down. *(Slight pause.)* I have to ask you something.

MARY: Anything.

LAINIE: Did you ever make out with Tommy Marcum?

MARY: What?!

LAINIE: Did you?

MARY: He was your boyfriend!

LAINIE: *(Crossing toward the sofa.)* I know. Did you ever make out with him?

MARY: *(Turning away.)* No.

LAINIE: *(Crossing behind sofa.)* Are you sure?

MARY: I would never do that while you were seeing him.

LAINIE: Aha — but you did when I went to away to college, didn't you?

MARY: *(Standing up and crossing right.)* Why are you asking me that?

LAINIE: *(Following Mary, grabbing a necktie from the "go" pile and wrapping it around her hands, threatening.)* Sonia told me the truth, but I didn't believe her.

MARY: What business was it of hers?

LAINIE: When I die, I'll automatically know the truth, you know, so you may as well tell me now . . .

(Lainie "catches" Mary around the waist with the tie upstage center, and laughs maniacally.)

MARY: *(Trying to free herself.)* Stop it! Besides, I was only sixteen.

LAINIE: *(Not letting Mary go, pulling the tie tighter.)* Ah — confession!

MARY: God, he was a creep anyway. He told all his stupid friends I wouldn't let him stick his hand down my pants . . .

LAINIE: Mary!

MARY: . . . *after* I slept with him.

LAINIE: *(Releasing the tie.)* You *slept* with him?!

MARY: Kidding!

LAINIE: Thank God.

MARY: Not even close. *(Pause.)* What made you think of that?

(Lainie crosses to her "keep" pile and holds up their high school yearbook.)

MARY: God, no!

LAINIE: Yes!

MARY: *(Reaching for the book.)* Give me that!

LAINIE: No!

MARY: That was the worst picture ever taken of me, ever!

LAINIE: *(Sitting down by her "keep" pile, right, and thumbing through the year-book.)* What page? Let me see . . .

(Something in an open box catches Mary's eye as she moves toward Lainie to grab the yearbook.)

MARY: Oh my God, you're going to like what I just found better.

LAINIE: What?

(Mary holds up the screwdriver.)

LAINIE: No way!

MARY: And look what else.

(Mary holds up a small teacup, the mate of the other, and, kneeling, places it on the box next to the first cup, center.)

It's a tea party after all.

(Lights fade to black.)

END OF PLAY

She's Fabulous

JACK NEARY

She's Fabulous was first presented as part of the Boston Theater Marathon of Ten-Minute plays on May 21, 2006. The play featured Ellen Colton as Clarice and Bobbie Steinbach as Bethel. It was directed by the author.

CHARACTERS
CLARICE
BETHEL

SETTING
A theater

• • •

In the black, we hear polite theater applause.
Lights up dimly on Clarice and Bethel, in theater seats, applauding politely.
Both ladies are over fifty, tastefully dressed for the theater.
> *The Lights rise fully. Each lady takes her theater playbill, opens it, and reads. This goes on for a reasonably uncomfortable amount of time. Finally, without looking up from the playbill, Clarice speaks.*

CLARICE: Well, she's fabulous.
BETHEL: *(Instantly, face still in playbill.)* She is.
> *(Another longish beat of playbill reading. Again, when they speak, the ladies' faces remain in the playbill.)*
CLARICE: The nuance. The poise.
BETHEL: The subtlety. The humor.
CLARICE: Everything. It's there.
BETHEL: Organic.
CLARICE: Yes. It's organic. From the gut.
BETHEL: Exactly. From the gut. It's as if she has lived her life in the gut. Of the character.
CLARICE: Astonishing.
BETHEL: Awesome.
> *(Beat.)*
> In the unabused sense of the word.
CLARICE: It's not her out there.
BETHEL: No, it's not.
> *(Beat.)*
> In other shows, it's her out there.
CLARICE: She's always her out there.
BETHEL: Always.
> *(Beat.)*
> I'm never me. Out there.
CLARICE: You're not.

BETHEL: You're never you.

CLARICE: I try not to be.

BETHEL: *(Beat.)* But she's always her. Out there.

CLARICE: Always.

> *(Beat.)*
> Except tonight.

BETHEL: *(Almost simultaneously.)* Except tonight.

> *(Beat.)*
> Awesome.

CLARICE: In the unabused sense.

BETHEL: Exactly.

> *(More playbill reading. They have yet to take their faces from the playbill since the lights came up.)*

CLARICE: And the growth! The growth of the character from lights up to intermission!

BETHEL: Awesome.

> *(Longer than usual beat.)*
> Awesome growth.
> *(The longest playbill read yet. Finally, Bethel closes her playbill and slaps it into her lap.)*

BETHEL: *(Continued.)* She should get a growth!

CLARICE: *(Also stops reading, slaps playbill to lap.)* A big growth! Painful! Large growth.

BETHEL: This is criminal!

CLARICE: *(Points toward "stage.")* That is MY part!

BETHEL: That is YOUR part!

CLARICE: Or your part.

BETHEL: Or my part.

CLARICE: So it's not just me.

BETHEL: It's not just you.

CLARICE: She's embarrassing, isn't she?

BETHEL: She's embarrassing. You look up *embarrassing* in the dictionary, there's no definition. Just her headshot.

CLARICE: The one with the blackhead!

BETHEL: She says it's a flaw in the negative.

CLARICE: It's a blackhead!

BETHEL: Of course it's a blackhead!

> *(They both instantly and energetically go back to the playbill. After a moment, Clarice slams the playbill shut again.)*

CLARICE: I prepared for that audition! I told you! I prepared!

BETHEL: You prepared! You're a preparer! Everybody knows that!

CLARICE: And you! You prepared!

BETHEL: Of course I prepared! You think I didn't prepare? I went to the cemetery. I took the script. I ordered it from Baker's. I memorized that scene standing at a gravestone! "Forgive me, Willy, I can't cry!" At a gravestone, I learned it! By heart!

CLARICE: In February!

BETHEL: At the grave of a perfect stranger! Jasper Hillenbrandt, 1919 to 1981. And his loving wife Joyce. Not dead yet, apparently. I picked him because the stone came up to my waist. Someplace to put the script. Freed up my hands. For expression.

CLARICE: *(Rhapsodically.)* Oh! When you express . . . !
(Couple of hand gestures.)

BETHEL: Nobody prepares like me! Tell me somebody who prepares like me!

CLARICE: Nobody prepares like you!

BETHEL: You prepare like me!

CLARICE: Except me. I prepare like you.

BETHEL: You prepared for that audition!

CLARICE: Of course I prepared!

BETHEL: Of course you did! Like me! I went to that cemetery!

CLARICE: I slept with that salesman!

BETHEL: Research!

CLARICE: Preparation!

BETHEL: That bitch!
(Both vehemently back to the playbill. Another moment. Pages are flipped, though there's very little reading being done now. Clarice slaps the playbill to her lap.)

CLARICE: The thing of it is . . .

BETHEL: *(Playbill down.)* What is the thing of it?

CLARICE: The thing of it is . . . the preparing. What's the point?

BETHEL: I see your point.

CLARICE: Did she prepare?

BETHEL: She never prepares.

CLARICE: Did she get the part?

BETHEL: She got the part.

CLARICE: She didn't prepare. She got the part. We DID prepare . . .

BETHEL: We don't even get comps.
(Silence. No playbill reading this time. Just contemplation.)

CLARICE: So . . . what do we say?

BETHEL: When?

CLARICE: Backstage. When it's over. We have to say something.

BETHEL: We say . . . congratulations.

CLARICE: Congratulations?

BETHEL: Congratulations. It's a very safe word to say after a show. You say it, she thinks you're saying congratulations on your performance. What you think to yourself is "Congratulations you got us to come see you in this piece of shit."

CLARICE: Will it work?

BETHEL: It always works.

CLARICE: *(Long beat; thinking.)* Huh.

BETHEL: What huh?

CLARICE: Congratulations. That's what you said to me after *Lost in Yonkers.*

BETHEL: Oh.

(To playbill.)

Did I?

CLARICE: You didn't like me in *Lost in Yonkers?*

BETHEL: Everybody liked you in *Lost in Yonkers.*

CLARICE: Are you everybody?

BETHEL: Am I ever everybody?

CLARICE: *(Beat.)* Oh. Oh, I get it. You wanted that part.

BETHEL: Why would I want that part? I'm way too young for that part.

CLARICE: And I'm not?

BETHEL: Apparently not.

CLARICE: I worked my butt off playing that part.

BETHEL: Yes. Yes, you did.

CLARICE: What do you mean, "Yes, yes, I did"?

BETHEL: You worked your butt off playing that part.

CLARICE: You saw the work? You're not supposed to see the work.

BETHEL: I saw the work. Forgive me.

CLARICE: You really saw it? You saw the work?

BETHEL: I did.

CLARICE: Seriously. You saw the work.

BETHEL: You were a thespian jackhammer out there.

CLARICE: And you could do better, I suppose.

BETHEL: Better? Who's to say? It's such a subjective thing with acting, isn't it. Better. Who's to judge who is better when playing a role. An actor makes a choice. Another actor makes another choice. Better? Who's to say? Now — would I have done it differently? Of course.

CLARICE: Differently?

BETHEL: Differently.

CLARICE: You would have been different playing that part?

BETHEL: Yes. I would have been different playing that part.

CLARICE: How? How would you have been different?

BETHEL: *(Beat.)* I would have been better.

CLARICE: *(Anger building.)* There is nothing you would have done different or better or anything else from me in that . . .

BETHEL: *(Stops her.)* What are we arguing? We have vitriol. We should waste it on each other?

CLARICE: Probably not.

BETHEL: No! We have vitriol! We should aim it in the right direction!

CLARICE: At the bitch with the blackhead!

BOTH: RIGHT!

(They go back to reading the playbills. As they do, the theater lights blink, indicating the intermission is nearing its end.)

CLARICE: Uh oh. Fasten your seat belts. Here comes the second act.

BETHEL: Maybe if we're lucky, Willy gets in the car early and runs her down in the driveway.

(They both chuckle playfully. They shush each other as the lights continue to dim. After a moment, they both put down their playbills and sigh wistfully.)

BETHEL: *(Continued.)* It's a beautiful part.

CLARICE: It is. It is.

BETHEL: She's so lucky.

CLARICE: Yep.

BETHEL: *(Beat.)* We'll tell her that. That's what we'll tell her.

CLARICE: What?

BETHEL: After the show. We'll tell her that it's a beautiful part. That's she's so lucky to be playing it.

CLARICE: We don't do congratulations?

BETHEL: No.

CLARICE: *(Beat.)* No.

(Beat.)

She's better than congratulations.

BETHEL: She is.

CLARICE: *(Longer beat.)* She's fabulous, isn't she?

BETHEL: She is.

CLARICE: *(Beat.)* Shit.

BETHEL: Yes.

(Beat.)

Shit.

CLARICE: *(Longer beat; lightbulb.)* Hey! We're not dead!

BETHEL: No, we're not.

CLARICE: Somebody else will do it.

BETHEL: Another theater. Another time.

CLARICE: We'll audition.

BETHEL: We will.

> *(The lights begin to dim. They settle in for the second act. Clarice takes Bethel's hand, squeezes it, and smiles.)*

CLARICE: We'll be fabulous!

> *(Bethel squeezes back. They both smile. The lights fade to black.)*

END OF PLAY

Pillow

FREDERICK STROPPEL

Pillow was first produced by the Theatre Artists Workshop of Westport in Norwalk, Connecticut, in July 2004, as part of their annual Word of the Week Festival. It was directed by June Walker Rogers and had the following cast:
Wilma — Betty Jinnette; Janice — Barbara Rhoades.

CHARACTERS
WILMA
JANICE

SETTING
An apartment

● ● ●

An apartment. There is a loud knocking at the door. Wilma comes out, wearing a bathrobe.

WILMA: I'm coming. Coming . . . !
(*Wilma opens the door. Janice enters, frazzled.*)
JANICE: Jesus, I need a drink, fast.
(*Janice heads straight over to the bar, and grabs a bottle of Scotch.*)
WILMA: Janice . . . ? What's the matter? Are you all right?
(*Janice pours herself a stiff drink, and drinks it in one gulp.*)
JANICE: Yeah, I'm just super.
(*Janice makes herself another drink.*)
WILMA: What time is it?
JANICE: It's late. Maybe three o'clock. Listen, do you have a spare pillow? I might have to sleep on your couch tonight.
WILMA: Certainly, if you need to . . .
(*Janice downs another glass.*)
My, you're drinking awfully fast. You might want to try the less expensive Scotch . . .
JANICE: No, two or three more of these and I'll be fine.
WILMA: What's going on, Janice?
JANICE: What's going on? Well, I have a bone to pick with you, Wilma. That guy you set me up with tonight? Eddie Gibson? That great catch, that ball of fire, that Mr. Wonderful?
WILMA: Oh, yes, your big date! How did it go?
JANICE: He's dead.
WILMA: Oh, dear. You didn't like him?
JANICE: No, he's *dead.* Kaput. Finito. A nonparticipant in the life experience.
WILMA: He's dead?
JANICE: Which really shouldn't surprise you, since the old coot was probably pushing ninety.
WILMA: Oh, he wasn't that old. I would say, on the far side of seventy.

JANICE: How could you stick me with that decrepit old dinosaur? I'm a vital woman in the prime of my life. I could go to any bar in this town and have my pick of guys half his age. Guys who, at this moment, are still very much alive.

WILMA: I'm sorry. Janice. I just thought, you being a nice single lady, and Mr. Gibson being a mature widower of means — it seemed like a good match.

JANICE: A good match? The fact that you could even consider hooking me up with old Methuselah up there . . . Sometimes I wonder if you really know who I am.

WILMA: You mean he's upstairs, in your room, right now?

JANICE: That's why I want to stay down here. I'm not spending the night with a corpse, thank you, regardless of how desperate *you* seem to think I am.

WILMA: What happened to him?

JANICE: I don't know, I'm not a doctor. One minute he's conscious, the next . . . Blooey.

(She sighs.)

I have no luck with men.

WILMA: Maybe he's asleep. He tends to nap a lot at the office.

JANICE: He's dead, Wilma. I've seen enough dead bodies in my life to know when somebody's kicked the bucket.

WILMA: You have?

JANICE: All I can think is, his heart must have exploded, because there was no advance warning. We were in bed, things were proceeding very nicely, he seemed to be enjoying himself . . .

WILMA: Wait a minute — you were in bed? You mean, you were . . . ?

JANICE: It's the middle of the night, Wilma, what did you think we were doing? Playing Par-cheesi?

WILMA: But I thought you didn't like him.

JANICE: Well, he's hardly my dream man, but once I got past the liver spots and the colostomy bag, I found him quite agreeable. Still, the next time you try to fix me up, I'd appreciate it if you'd pick somebody who's likely to last the night.

WILMA: Dear me. Have you called the police?

JANICE: Not yet. Because I know they're going to ask a lot of questions. Watch, they're gonna try to say I was involved somehow.

WILMA: Well, you *were* involved, Janice. I mean, if you were "doing something" with him at the time . . .

JANICE: That was just a coincidence. I've had plenty of men in my day, and this is the first one who ever died under me.

WILMA: Under you? You mean you were *on top* of him?

JANICE: *(Drily.)* Yes, Wilma, I was on top. We have the vote now, you know. Our options have expanded.

WILMA: But I mean — sitting and bouncing on a man his age . . .

JANICE: Well, I wasn't going to wait for him to climb up on me. It took him ten minutes just to take off his shoes.

WILMA: It just strikes me as rather bold, for a first date. I've been married to Vernon some twenty-six years now, and I *never* . . .

JANICE: Well, maybe you should. A little empowerment once in a while would do you a world of good. It's a new century, Wilma. You don't have to just lie there with your eyes closed and recite the multiplication tables to yourself anymore. Get yourself a pair of spurs and ride that bad boy.

WILMA: *(Embarrassed.)* Gracious, we shouldn't be talking about such naughty things, not with poor Mr. Gibson dead up there.

JANICE: Yeah, it's a fucking shame. Oh, well.

(She pours herself another drink.)

WILMA: And you say it happened suddenly? That's a blessing.

JANICE: Yeah, I took the pillow off his face, and he was all blue, his eyes were bulging, his tongue was swollen . . . It really took the air out of my balloon, let me tell you.

WILMA: *(Bewildered.)* There was a pillow over his face?

JANICE: *(Nods.)* I was holding it there. That's why I didn't know he was dead until well after the fact.

WILMA: *(Shocked.)* You were holding a pillow over Mr. Gibson's face?

JANICE: It's a little bedroom trick I picked up. See, when you cut off the air supply during sex, it intensifies the orgasm ten times over. You and Vernon really should try it. When it works, it's spectacular.

WILMA: But — Janice — for Heaven's sake, you must have suffocated him!

JANICE: Oh, I don't think so. I've done the pillow routine lots of times, I never lost anybody before. One guy went into a semi-coma, but he had asthma, I found out later. Now I always ask beforehand.

WILMA: But didn't you notice anything? Didn't you see Mr. Gibson struggling, or waving his arms?

JANICE: He couldn't wave his arms. They were tied to the bedposts.

WILMA: His arms were tied to the bedposts?

JANICE: And his legs. Spread-eagled, is the technical term.

WILMA: *(Outraged.)* You tied up Mr. Gibson?

JANICE: You know, there's an unpleasant moral tone creeping into your voice. Yes, I tied up Mr. Gibson. Do you have a problem with that?

WILMA: My God! That poor old man . . . !

JANICE: Oh, he loved it, are you kidding? We were having a blast until he croaked.

WILMA: I have to say, Janice, if I'd known that you favored such strange unsavory practices . . .

JANICE: What do you mean, strange? These are common sexual techniques familiar to any modern American woman. Don't you ever watch cable?

WILMA: Maybe I've led a sheltered life, but I can't believe that smothering someone while you bounce around on his privates is a popular form of sexplay, even in New York.

JANICE: All right, the pillow thing is a little more exotic. That's something I picked up on my own, back when I was a hooker.

WILMA: *(Shocked.)* You were a hooker?

JANICE: Well — an escort. I had my own phone number. It was just a youthful phase I was going through, when I was supporting my drug habit.

WILMA: You had a drug habit?

JANICE: A small one. Not heroin or anything. Just a little coke here, a little crack there. I kicked it no sweat when I was in prison.

WILMA: You were in prison?

JANICE: I don't like talking about that. It was a bullshit charge; I was practically innocent. Anyway, my cell mate, a very lovely woman, helped me get clean. And since she was a rather assertive lesbian, I wound up repaying her in dribs and drabs. But I learned a lot about myself in the process, and I have no regrets.

WILMA: I had no idea you had such a colorful past.

JANICE: Well, you see, that's my point. If you'd taken the time to really get to know me, then you would know what kind of man to set me up with. It's a very tricky business, bringing people together.

WILMA: If I'd known you were into kinky perverted things like that, I wouldn't have tried to set you up at all. We obviously travel in wildly different circles.

JANICE: Everybody's into things like that, Wilma. Everybody but you. You think your precious Mr. Gibson was some kind of altar boy? He's the one who wanted to get tied up, you know. He's the one who brought out the maraschino cherries. And you know what else he did?

WILMA: I don't want to know.

JANICE: He took out his teeth and gummed my toes.

WILMA: *(Gags.)* Ewww!

JANICE: That's right — sucked the paint right off my nails. So don't be so cocksure about what's normal and what isn't. I'll tell you what's not normal — being married to the same guy for twenty-six years, doing the same boring things day after day, never getting on top. I'll bet you don't own a single piece of rubber latex.

WILMA: *(Thinks a moment.)* No, I don't.

JANICE: You're hopelessly out of the loop, Wilma. I should set *you* up. I know a couple of guys who could really blow some fresh air up your schmatta. For a price, of course.

WILMA: I appreciate that, Janice, but I'm perfectly happy the way things are.

(Beat.)

At least I think I am.

JANICE: It's your life, Shirley Temple.

(Janice polishes off her drink.)

WILMA: Well, I think it's time we called the police about Mr. Gibson, don't you?

JANICE: Yeah, I guess I should go up and scrape the candle wax off him.

(Janice starts to leave.)

WILMA: You know, Janice —

JANICE: Yeah?

WILMA: I would love to hear more about your lesbian experiences some day.

JANICE: *(Smiles.)* I'll get my pillow.

(Janice exits.)

END OF PLAY

Jump Shot

GREG ZITTEL

Jump Shot was originally done at Cincinnati's Performing Arts School, under the direction of David Rothko. Maria Funcheon played Betty, Lamicah Thomas played Jenny.

CHARACTERS
BETTY

JENNY

SETTING
Betty's room

*   *   *

Betty sits at her computer. Her friend Jenny is working out the kinks in her jump shot.

BETTY: Stop you're making me nervous.

JENNY: There's something wrong with my form, I don't think I'm getting enough backspin on my ten footer.

BETTY: You're bothering me.

JENNY: You're not doing anything, relax.

BETTY: Are you outta your mind?

JENNY: It's a computer.

BETTY: I know what it is.

JENNY: So don't make a mountain out of a molehill.

BETTY: You got SAT scores to beat the band and you're averaging eleven points a game you'll go to college and it won't cost your parents a penny.

JENNY: You'll get into college.

BETTY: If I don't find one I like I'll end up somewhere I don't want to go, I've gotta stay ahead of this.

JENNY: Where do you want to go?

BETTY: Yale, Princeton, Harvard.

JENNY: What were your SATs?

BETTY: Forget it.

JENNY: What did you get?

BETTY: Mariah Carey could score better than I did.

JENNY: She can score anything she wants.

BETTY: You think she even took them?

JENNY: How would I know?

BETTY: What do you think she got?

JENNY: I don't know, 36 D.

BETTY: I don't want my parents to get involved.

JENNY: There a problem?

BETTY: Of course. If it's left to them I'll end up in The Christian College of Suffocation and Occasional Beatings.

JENNY: That's not good.

BETTY: Of course not.

JENNY: What are you looking for in a college?

BETTY: What I should be looking for, cute guys and easy classes.

JENNY: That worries me.

BETTY: What?

JENNY: Sometimes I wonder if I should lower my percentages.

BETTY: What do you mean?

JENNY: How can I get a hunk if I'm dropping jumpers better than most guys?

BETTY: You're being so self-centered, think about me for a minute.

JENNY: Do you have any ideas?

BETTY: Of where I want to go to school?

JENNY: No, mixing concrete.

BETTY: I was thinking of the University of Miami.

JENNY: Florida?

BETTY: Yeah.

JENNY: Do you think you can get in there?

BETTY: How hard can it be?

JENNY: What do you know about the school?

BETTY: You can take basket weaving and they played East Carolina in football.

JENNY: Sounds like you could get in.

BETTY: Maybe I should apply to East Carolina.

JENNY: Where is East Carolina?

BETTY: Don't be dumb. It's "East — Carolina" that means it's in east Carolina.

JENNY: *(She has to think about that.)* Well, do you know anything about it?

BETTY: My father graduated there, I know that.

JENNY: Oh.

BETTY: Yeah, can't be hard to get in.

JENNY: Did your mother go to college, maybe you should look where she went.

BETTY: No, she's a nurse, nurses don't go to college.

JENNY: Where do they go?

BETTY: Somewhere close to where doctors go.

JENNY: I think Miami sounds good.

BETTY: Yeah, me too. You say Miami, I hear South Beach.

JENNY: What's that?

BETTY: Sin city.

(They laugh.)

JENNY: Really?

BETTY: That's the way I read it.

JENNY: You read about it?

BETTY: I read about it in *Parade* magazine, they said that's where Britney Spears, Little Missy, and Jennifer Lopez go.

JENNY: What were they doing there?

BETTY: There was a concert.

JENNY: Cool. Three ho's and a show.

BETTY: Funny. But I'm serious.

> *(Betty is starry-eyed.)*
>
> It's warm, there's the beach for tanning, hot shops along the strip, and it's supposedly the number-one party school in America.

JENNY: What would you major in?

BETTY: Who cares?

JENNY: Nobody.

BETTY: Why do we have to go to college?

JENNY: To get an education, duh.

BETTY: That seems so old-fashioned.

JENNY: You think?

BETTY: Where did Madonna, Lil' Kim, or any of the girls on *American Idol* go?

JENNY: I'll bet not one of them graduated college and they're all making the big bucks.

BETTY: Yeah, but you can play basketball, you're set. What can I do?

JENNY: You look good.

BETTY: You gotta have a skill. If I don't get a jump shot, I'll have no shot at all.

JENNY: Don't be depressing, you have all the makings of a successful life.

BETTY: Name one thing other than my boobs.

JENNY: Oh stop. You're smart.

BETTY: I got lousy SATs.

JENNY: You do have a great body.

BETTY: Women can work now, you have to have a skill, not a body.

> *(They think a moment.)*
>
> What could my skill be?

JENNY: You go out with the hottest guy in school.

BETTY: Making out in a pickup doesn't rate as a skill.

JENNY: *(Take herself seriously.)* Tell me something.

BETTY: What?

JENNY: Honest?

BETTY: Sure what?

JENNY: You still a virgin?

BETTY: Absolutely.

JENNY: Well if you can date him, make out in his pickup parked on the byways of Ohio, and remain a virgin — you must have skill.

BETTY: You got a point there.

JENNY: Guys are the genius'. They can get from first base to third before a girl has two balls on her.

(They laugh.)

BETTY: Don't be making jokes, I gotta figure this college thing out.

JENNY: What about Miami, I thought you settled on going there.

BETTY: No, I said it looked good. I have to have a reach school, three possibles and a pathetic dump.

JENNY: I haven't done any of that stuff yet.

BETTY: No, that's what I'm saying — They're coming to you.

JENNY: I did hear from a couple of schools and when the season is over they said they'd probably make me an offer.

BETTY: Where?

JENNY: Connecticut, Tennessee, and Ohio State.

BETTY: Ahhhhhh! They're gonna offer you scholarships?

JENNY: That's what they said.

BETTY: Oh my God, where do you want to go? Which one do you think you would rather take?

JENNY: Do I really want to play basketball?

BETTY: Jenny baby, you're so good.

JENNY: Yeah, but I just fell into it, I started doing it and it turned out it was easy.

BETTY: What are you saying?

JENNY: I don't really like it.

BETTY: I never woulda known, the way you push the ball around, scoring, rebounding, you're so good.

JENNY: And blocking shots.

BETTY: And blocking shots.

JENNY: Stealing the ball.

BETTY: Stealing.

JENNY: Full-court passes on fast breaks.

BETTY: Stop it!

JENNY: But do I really want a scholarship to college where you eat, sleep and drink basketball? That's what those schools want.

BETTY: Who cares if you like it or not, you get a scholarship you take it, don't you?

JENNY: Do you?

BETTY: I would.

JENNY: You would?

BETTY: Sure that would end my worries.

JENNY: No it wouldn't. You want to tan, stand on the beach in Miami, and see if any guys flirt.

BETTY: *(Swooning.)* College must be great.

JENNY: But if you had a scholarship for basketball you couldn't do any of that, because there'd always be more practice, weight training, games.

BETTY: You make it sound like they own you.

JENNY: When they give you a basketball scholarship they do own you.

BETTY: No downtime?

JENNY: No, not the way I hear it. No downtime, no, none.

   (Realizes what has happened.)

   I was just standing there a minute ago practicing my jump shot, while you were worrying about college. Oh brother!

BETTY: And I was wishing I had a jump shot so I didn't have to worry about college.

JENNY: I'll give you my basketball scholarship if you give me four years of wearing new bikinis, standing on a beach checking out the guys who are doing the checking, and dancing at the hot South Beach clubs.

BETTY: Well, when you put it that way.

JENNY: Sure, what's college about?

BETTY: What is it about?

JENNY: It's about life.

BETTY: Everybody makes it seem like life is about college.

JENNY: You got that right.

BETTY: Meeting somebody on a beach is more promising than meeting somebody on a girl's basketball team.

JENNY: See what I'm saying?

BETTY: Yeah. I don't wanna go out with somebody named Lucy.

JENNY: Me either. I mean don't get me wrong, it's alright for them, if that's what makes 'em happy.

BETTY: Not in my pickup.

JENNY: *(Forlorn.)* I don't know what to do.

BETTY: Me either.

JENNY: I'm a mess.

BETTY: Me too.

JENNY: What is this all about?

BETTY: Of course, some people actually like studying.

JENNY: Some actually like basketball.

BETTY: I don't know.

JENNY: Me either.

BETTY: We gotta figure this out.

JENNY: You mean life, right?

BETTY: Exactly.

(The two sit together, thinking . . . Lights come down . . .)

END OF PLAY

PLAYS FOR
TWO
MEN

The 11:05

Liz Amberly

The 11:05 was originally produced by Algonquin Productions
for the Samuel French Off-Off Broadway Festival and
The American Globe Theatre Turnip Theatre Fifteen Minute
Play Festival (Winner, Audience Favorite). It was directed
by Thomas Cote, and the cast was as follows:
Mark — Michael J. Reilly; Ray — Jed Dickson.

CHARACTERS
MARK: young, uptight businessman
RAY: age open, but older than Mark, union worker

SETTING
A train platform

•   •   •

Two men on a train platform in a small suburban town. Ray sits calmly on the bench. Mark is pacing along the deserted platform shouting into his cell phone.

MARK: *(Into the phone.)* . . . I'm standing here missing it! You hear that? . . . And now it's gone! Gone!! If you get this message, call me the hell back. Ten thirty-five, that's the next train.
(He hangs up.)
RAY: It's eleven-oh-five.
MARK: What, the time? Ten-oh-six.
RAY: No. Next train. Eleven-oh-five.
MARK: The trains run every half hour.
RAY: Half-hour till ten-oh-five; then every hour till three. Check the schedule.
MARK: Damn it.
RAY: Eleven-oh—
MARK: *(Stopping him, still distracted.)* — I heard you thanks. Great. Now we might not make it.
RAY: *(Moving over on the bench to make room.)* Want a seat?
MARK: No thanks.
(Mark paces and dials his cell. Ray pulls out a tiny bottle of booze — the kind from an airplane — and takes a drink.)
MARK: *(Continued.) (Into the phone.)* Turns out the next train's eleven-oh-five. I'm on the eastbound platform off of Lakeside Hill. You better be on your way.
(He hangs up.)
RAY: Some people are just late sometimes.
MARK: *(Checking his pockets.)* What happened to my lighter? Oh, man . . . ! — Hey, you got a light?
RAY: *(He holds out the mini-bottle.)* Sorry. Want some a this?
MARK: Uh, no thanks. *(Then, to himself, about the lighter . . .)* . . . Come on!
RAY: Ya don't have to share. See?

(He pulls out more unopened little bottles.)

MARK: I don't need a drink at ten o'clock in the morning.

RAY: You need somethin'. You seem kinda uptight.

MARK: Yeah, well —

RAY: Like super, mega uptight. You gotta chill out.

MARK: I need to get to a meeting, OK?

(Ray's cell phone rings.)

. . . Your phone.

RAY: It's like they all gotta call me and remind me what day it is. Like I don't know.

MARK: If you're not going to answer it, you should turn it off.

(Ray turns it off.)

MARK: *(Continued.)* So, are you waiting for a train or just hanging out?

RAY: Waitin' for a train. The eleven-oh-five.

MARK: But you were sitting right here. You could've taken the ten-oh-five.

RAY: Could've, but missed it. Spent more days'n I can count waitin' for Joey who never caught a mode of transportation in his life. Like if I say "Let's take a bus" I gotta calculate which one we can afford to miss so we can catch another one that still gets us there on time.

MARK: You're telling me you show up early, knowing you're not going to make it?

RAY: Gotta wait for Joey, just like you gotta wait for what's-his-face.

MARK: Yeah, well, this guy's a pain in the ass. He's got all this tech stuff — computer whiz — but for the biggest meeting in his life, he can't even manage a simple cell phone call to tell me he's running late. Idiot!

(Fiddles with his cigarette. Then puts it away.)

And now I can't even have a smoke.

RAY: The closest store's over on Mulberry if you want matches.

MARK: If I leave to go get matches, Dickson'll show up and think I went without him.

(He sits down.)

See, we've got this meeting. Dickson's got the hardware. I've got the tickets. And if we don't land this account, we've got nothing.

RAY: You sound like Joey . . . "Gotta plan, Gotta go. Gotta get there." — Of course, in the end he'd screw up whatever plan it was, that's Joey's way.

MARK: You mean like he never showed up?

RAY: Oh, he showed up. But stuff would go wrong. Like, one time he says we gotta go to D.C. and root against the Redskins on their own field. So we're waiting on the platform what seems like hours — And then in the end he's like saying "I got to take a leak, you think we got time? It's seven minutes."

(He bursts out laughing.)

Seven minutes and now he's wondering if he should piss yet.

MARK: Did you make the train?

RAY: Missed it. And not just him. Me! Like I'm such a jerk that I gotta wait for my buddy who can't find the toilet.

(Ray laughs. Mark checks his phone, which is silent.)

MARK: Where the hell is he? Man, this guy's always trying to screw me.

RAY: Or maybe he's just —

MARK: This project was my idea, and now he's not going to show and make us both look bad.

RAY: Well, it could still work out. There was another game in Dallas —

MARK: — This isn't a football game, OK? If we ruin this meeting, it very seriously might lose me my job. So, just don't act like you know what's going on. — God, I need a cigarette!!

(Ray's cell phone rings again.)

Shut that thing up!!

RAY: Maybe it's your worker friend. Callin' me. If I was somebody who knew what you was like, I'd rather talk to me, too.

(This cracks him up.)

MARK: Or maybe somebody's trying to reach you like I'm trying to reach Dickson, and you're being an ass about it, just like he is.

(Ray gets out some old travel brochures and tickets, arranging them on the bench next to him. Mark paces. He dials. Nothing. He dials another number. Nothing.)

RAY: *(Pulls out another bottle.)* I'm still offerin'.

MARK: No thanks. — You know what . . . yeah, OK. They're little. Can I pay you something?

RAY: You think I'm a bum? I work. Union. Probably make more'n you.

MARK: Probably.

RAY: How much you make?

MARK: After today, probably nothing.

RAY: Here, it's yours.

(Handing him an unopened bottle.)

. . . But you got to promise me somethin'.

MARK: Uh-oh. Promise you what?

RAY: You got a passport?

MARK: What?

RAY: Not on ya. You got a passport in your house?

MARK: Um, yeah.

RAY: You should pull it out. You seem like a guy who could use a vacation.

MARK: A couple years ago, my kid brother said we should go skiing in Switzerland. He broke his leg. Vacation before that was Mexico. He wanted to explore the Aztec ruins. But he ended up getting food poisoning, the runs, and sunburn. Not exactly picture perfect.

RAY: But did ya have any fun?

MARK: Some yeah, but he always acts irresponsible, so I don't even bother going anymore.

RAY: *(Pointing to some of his tickets.)* See how many places me and Joey got to? *(Ray's cell phone rings.)*

MARK: Maybe it's your buddy. You can't keep letting it ring.

RAY: *(Answers the phone and talks into it.)* Hello? . . . Yeah, I'm comin'. I'm takin' the eleven-oh-five. OK. See ya soon.
(Ray hangs up.)

MARK: Joey?

RAY: His widow.

MARK: Oh . . . Sorry. I didn't know —

RAY: Yeah, well . . .
(They both look out, not knowing what to say.)

MARK: You OK?

RAY: Yeah. Sure.
(There's a pause as they drink.)

RAY: Got these little bottles for free, ya know. When you travel a lot, you can make friends at the airport and they get you stuff from the airlines. You should think about it. Travelin'.

MARK: OK, say hypothetically, I was going to travel someplace. Where would be a place I should go? Like of all your vacations, which was the most fun?

RAY: I'd say Costa Rica. — You don't need to go tickin' off landmarks from a guidebook ta have a blast in Costa Rica. The best part was tryin' to get home. Joey says he'll return the car, and he comes in later, finds me at the bar, asking like "What's goin' on?" I say, "Missed it, dude." . . . And he gets all pissed off, like he thought they were gonna to hold the plane for him.

MARK: So you missed another one.

RAY: The next plane is like five hours later, and this guy at the bar chimes in about this mountain nearby where there's a party goin on. So we go. Got drunk off my ass. But then, you gotta know, in the end, we're racing to the airport and gotta fly through customs. But we made it. Yeah. — But

only cause we missed the first one. Joey always had to miss somethin'
before he'd make the next one. Always.

MARK: So, um, you said he died and all. Has he been gone a long time?

RAY: A year.

MARK: Oh. Hey, I'm sorry.

RAY: Yeah. Problem is, kept tellin' 'em it didn't happen.

MARK: It's hard to accept when someone —

RAY: No. See, cause it couldn't a happened. No way. — The thing is, I know
Joey. He was comin' back from his cousin's weddin', and I went ta pick
him up at the airport.

MARK: And he never showed up?

RAY: They said it was mechanical failure. Crashed. . . . But I heard what happened, and I'm sayin' he's not on it. There's no way he's there, cause that
woulda meant that he was on time. He never was on time for a plane in
his life.

MARK: But he was on this one

RAY: I didn't believe it. I watched the monitors. And people are tellin' me, but
I said he wasn't there. It's like I'm ready to yell at this guy who starts tryin'
to comfort me because he just doesn't know my friend. Joey woulda found
a way to be late that day. I know it.

MARK: So when'd you find out? That he was on it.

RAY: Well, first of all, his wife had a funeral.

MARK: So they at least recovered the body.

RAY: But there was not even gonna be an open casket, so how'd I know it was
gonna be him? So I said forget it and didn't go.

MARK: You didn't go to the funeral?

RAY: Nope. And now it's like a whole year later, and his wife's havin' a big thing
for this first anniversary of his death. Like we all should bring flowers to
his grave site and have some poems or songs or shit like that. Yeah, so,
anyway, that's happening today.

MARK: Hey, well . . . it's good that you're going this time. Really.
(He gets out his cell.)
I still don't know what's happening with Dickson.
(Dials his cell phone. Gets someone on the other end.)
. . . Hi, God I'm so glad I caught you! Your hubby's not answering his
cell; is he home? — what??? . . . no I'm at the train station. — Well of
course I was going, why wouldn't I be going? . . . But are you sure you
saw him get on?? Oh my God . . . Oh my God . . .
(He hangs up.)

RAY: He's missing it?

MARK: He told his wife I wanted out of the project, and he took an earlier train without me. Nine-oh-five. Three trains ago!!!

RAY: So call ahead and let the clients know you're on your way.

MARK: . . . Yeah.

(Dials as fast as he can, talking to himself.)

. . . Oh, man, Dickson, you cannot screw me out of this . . . If you tell them I'm out, I will kill you. Do you hear me . . . I will kill you!!

(Then listens into the phone.)

Nothing.

(Hangs up, then screams out.)

Dickson, You scum bag shithead!! — Do you know what this means? He's out with them touring the sites without me. He's making sure I'm eliminated. Piece of shit! — Hey . . .

(Reaches out to RAY.)

. . . give me some of those bottles. Give me all of 'em! I'm goin' to get drunk and kill somebody! Here, give me some of those bottles . . .

RAY: You gotta watch yourself when you say you're gonna kill somebody.

MARK: I'm not gonna kill somebody.

RAY: I don't want to be responsible.

MARK: I just blow off steam, but really, I just think it'll help today if I get very, very plastered.

RAY: Plastered can be good sometimes. — Here. Guys like that got no place usin' up your time.

(He hands him a bottle.)

MARK: Thanks. You know, I always hated this stupid job anyway. Whether I get fired or not, I say screw the job.

RAY: That's it, screw the job!

(They toast.)

MARK: Well at least now I can go buy a lighter and finally have this smoke.

RAY: *(Pulling out a pack of matches.)* . . . Here. Use this.

MARK: I thought you said you didn't have any matches.

RAY: Yeah, that's what I said.

MARK: But you had matches the whole time.

RAY: Right.

MARK: You offered me booze but won't give me a light?

RAY: See, remember my story about Costa Rica? These are matches from that bar. Had 'em with me today, cause I was gonna give 'em to his wife. Somethin' from our favorite trip.

MARK: Well, of course you have to give them to her.

RAY: It just seems like maybe I'm not going to see her after all.

MARK: But you're going on the train.

RAY: I've been sayin' that since yesterday. See, I was supposed to sleep over night there.

MARK: But you can still make it. — Here, take the matches back. I'll get some.

RAY: People'll probably be all pissed off if I don't show . . . But I don't know if I can get on. Earlier today I thought I was goin' to do it, but it don't seem likely anymore.

MARK: Maybe if you stop drinking.

RAY: You mighta come out with that advice a little sooner.

MARK: It's not too late. Just . . . let me get you some coffee.

RAY: So I can get all high-strung like you? I hate coffee.

MARK: OK, so no coffee, but just promise me you're going to go.

RAY: Maybe if you made sure I got on.

MARK: Sorry —

RAY: Look at this . . . a free stocked bar while you wait. And matches if you need that cigarette.

MARK: So now you're going to bribe me?

RAY: Somehow it's easier when you're not the only one getting on.

MARK: But I've got to go and figure out what I'm going to do about my job and my life.

RAY: Well, when you're thinking about what you're gonna do when you're unemployed . . . don't forget to plan that vacation. You really should take your kid brother. He sounds fun.

MARK: If you like hanging out in emergency rooms.

RAY: He likes doin' stuff with ya; you gotta loosen up about the rest.

MARK: If I promise to take my brother somewhere, will you promise get on the next train when it comes?

RAY: I just gotta do it: get on the train.

MARK: You will.

(He begins to leave.)

RAY: I hope so.

MARK: *(Pause.)* . . . If I . . . stay, you will. If I make sure you . . . get on that train. — Now, I'm not going to take the train with you . . . But . . .

(He takes a moment before continuing.)

. . . I'll make sure you get on . . . Does that sound OK?

RAY: Yeah.

MARK: And if you go to this thing, I promise I'll take my kid brother some-where.

RAY: Yeah, hang out with the guys ya like.

MARK: Yeah. Hey, I appreciate the booze.

RAY: Want another one?

MARK: Maybe in a minute.

RAY: Good. — Shouldn't be too much longer. For the train.

MARK: *(Sits.)* Yeah. Not too long.

RAY: Right.

(*Referring to his brochures.*)

Look at this one. Now, that was a good trip too. You might check that out sometime.

(*Ray hands Mark the brochure as the lights fade.*)

END OF PLAY

Blue Skies

MARVIN L. COTLAR

*In life we have choices. For instance, we can
either do nothing . . . or we can paint.*

CHARACTERS

THE PAINTER: a male . . . or female, preferably over the age of thirty, but not younger than twenty-five.

THE MAN: preferably over the age of thirty, but not younger than twenty-five.

TIME

Daytime. Spring.

SETTING

Outside. Anywhere.

The stage is enveloped — sides, rear and above — by "gray sky." The sky is streaked with long and uneven swathes of various shades of blue, as if someone had been haphazardly painting here and there, perhaps sampling colors. (The above may be freely interpreted or may dispensed with entirely in favor of an empty stage.)

Downstage center a tall stepladder faces the audience. A paint-splattered paint can sits on its shelf.

Upstage, lying on the stage floor, are a stepladder; a half-dozen paint cans with dried paint splattered down their sides; a paintbrush; a pair of neatly folded, clean, white coveralls; and a clean, white painter's cap.

• • •

At the Rise: Paint brush in hand, The Painter stands on an upper step of a stepladder facing the audience. He (or she) absentmindedly HUMS "Blue Skies" as he or she "paints the sky." A Man enters, looks around, and stares up at The Painter. Drably dressed in suit and tie, The Man is generally morose. The Painter looks down at The Man and nods. The Man feebly nods back. The Painter resumes painting. The Man stares around aimlessly and coughs. Again, The Painter looks at him, smiles and resumes painting. The Man coughs again, a bit louder.

THE PAINTER: What?

THE MAN: Sorry, was nothing.

THE PAINTER: Oh, OK.

(The Painter resumes painting. The Man watches for a beat, then coughs a third time, louder yet.

THE PAINTER: What'd you say.

THE MAN: Sorry, just coughed. Sorry to disturb you.

(As the The Painter paints, The Man looks around and then back up at The Painter and stares at him for a long beat.)

THE MAN: *(Calling out.)* So, how are things up there?

(The Painter doesn't seem to hear The Man and continues painting.)

THE MAN: *(Louder.)* I say, how are things up there?

THE PAINTER: *(Looks around, then at The Man.)* Oh, what? You?

THE MAN: Up there. How are —

THE PAINTER: Up here?

THE MAN: Yep, how are things up there?

THE PAINTER: Same as down there, I suppose.

THE MAN: Hmm, you think so?

THE PAINTER: Well, now that you mention it . . .

(Contemplates for a moment.)

So, you tell me, how are things down there?

(The Man tentatively surveys the area around and about where he's standing, looks up at the sky and then deliberates for a moment longer.)

THE MAN: *(Doleful, with resignation.)* Gray. Down here things are definitely gray.

THE PAINTER: You think so?

THE MAN: For sure. But, the sky up there is certainly blue.

(The Painter smiles at The Man broadly. The Man nods. Then . . .)

THE MAN: Hmm, perhaps you can — No, never . . .

THE PAINTER: What? Tell me, maybe I —

THE MAN: *(Turns his head away.)* . . . Mind.

THE PAINTER: As you wish.

(The Painter resumes painting; The Man watches for a long beat.)

THE MAN: So, exactly what are you doing up there?

THE PAINTER: What does it look like? What are you doing down there?

THE MAN: *(Shrugs, weakly.)* Nothing.

THE PAINTER: *(Hand cupped to his ear.)* What did you say?

THE MAN: *(Shouts.)* NOTHING!

THE PAINTER: Well, that's certainly not anything to shout about.

(The Man looks away sheepishly. The Painter resumes painting, then looks at The Man and smiles. The Man again studies The Painter for a beat.)

THE MAN: So, you're just painting, that's it?!

(Again, The Painter smiles at The Man. The Man shakes his head in mild frustration. The Painter paints.)

THE MAN: Nothing but blue skies from now on, huh?

(The Painter shrugs, smiles.)

THE MAN: *(With faux curiosity.)* Skies were gray, but they're not going to be gray anymore, right?

(The Painter smiles again.)

THE MAN: Hmm.

(The Man surveys the sky, sighs.)

THE MAN: Doing this long?

THE PAINTER: Seems like forever.

THE MAN: A lot to do?

THE PAINTER: Keeps me busy.

THE MAN: You'll never finish.

THE PAINTER: Am I supposed to?

THE MAN: Finish?

THE PAINTER: Isn't that what you asked?

THE MAN: I didn't ask.

THE PAINTER: No, I asked.

THE MAN: Asked what?

THE PAINTER: If I'm supposed to finish.

THE MAN: I don't think you're going to.

THE PAINTER: I've got plenty of time.

THE MAN: How long?

THE PAINTER: Don't really know.

THE MAN: Days sure seem to be hurrying by.

THE PAINTER: Haven't noticed, been too busy.

THE MAN: Doing what?

THE PAINTER: What do you think?

THE MAN: *(Shrugs.)* That's what I asked you.

(The Painter stares at The Man, smiles, resumes painting.)

THE MAN: Why?

THE PAINTER: It's what I do.

THE MAN: Is it fun?

THE PAINTER: It's alright.

THE MAN: You could leave the sky gray, you know.

(The Painter shrugs. The Man reflects for a moment.)

THE MAN: Say, you get paid?

THE PAINTER: Not for this.

THE MAN: Then, why do you do it?

THE PAINTER: *(Shakes his head.)* What else would you have me do?

THE MAN: What?

THE PAINTER: I said, what else would you have me do?

(The Man shrugs.)

THE PAINTER: Then I'll just continue what I'm doing. What about you?

(*The Man is indifferent, studies the sky. Contemplates. Then, suddenly . . .*)

THE MAN: What's your favorite shade?

THE PAINTER: Of what?

THE MAN: Why blue, of course.

(*The Painter indicates he doesn't know or care.*)

THE MAN: Robin's Egg?

THE PAINTER: No.

THE MAN: Cornflower?

(*The Painter shakes his head.*)

THE MAN: Steel? Slate?

THE PAINTER: Neither.

THE MAN: Diamond? Maybe navy?

(*The Painter shakes his/her head.*)

THE MAN: Royal?

THE PAINTER: Definitely not royal.

THE MAN: Midnight?

THE PAINTER: It's not that late already, is it?

THE MAN: Not yet.

THE PAINTER: Then what time is it?

THE MAN: I don't know, but it could be late.

THE PAINTER: Late? Hmm.

THE MAN: It could be.

THE PAINTER: Then I'd better hurry.

(*As The Painter paints with single-mindedness, The Man ponders the sky. Finally . . .*)

THE MAN: How about sky?

THE PAINTER: Sky?

THE MAN: Sky blue, the color?

THE PAINTER: How about it?

THE MAN: Well, if you're painting the sky . . .

THE PAINTER: Who said that's what I'm doing?

THE MAN: Well, aren't you?

THE PAINTER: Haven't thought much about it.

THE MAN: Then, why are you doing it?

THE PAINTER: I thought I told you, things were gray.

THE MAN: But they're not gray anymore?

THE PAINTER: Nice, isn't it?

THE MAN: I know what you mean.

THE PAINTER: Nothin' but blue skies from now on.

THE MAN: How did you —

THE PAINTER: Good luck came a knocking at my door.

THE MAN: Is that why you paint?

THE PAINTER: What do you think?

(*The Man shrugs.*)

THE PAINTER: Gray skies, all of them gone.

THE MAN: (*A bit astonished.*) It really works?

THE PAINTER: Why not give it a try?

(*The Man stares vacantly at The Painter. Ponders for a long beat.*)

THE PAINTER: Well?

THE MAN: I've never . . .

THE PAINTER: Got to start sometime.

THE MAN: What if I make a mistake?

THE PAINTER: Don't know until you try. Besides, there's plenty of paint.

THE MAN: I'm afraid.

THE PAINTER: No need to be.

THE MAN: Well . . .

THE PAINTER: You only have so much time.

(*The Man shrugs, shakes his head.*)

THE PAINTER: Like you said, days are hurrying by.

THE MAN: Must admit, I never saw things looking so right.

THE PAINTER: There's a ladder in back. Paint, too.

MAN: Can I think about it?

(*The Painter smiles at The Man. Resumes painting. The Man mulls things over for a beat.*)

THE MAN: Are you sure?

THE PAINTER: Plenty of sky for both of us.

(*Hand to his chin, The Man reflects, studies The Painter, studies the sky.*)

THE PAINTER: It's up to you, your choice.

THE MAN: What's the alternative again?

THE PAINTER: Gray skies?

(*The Man deliberates for several beats more. Then cautiously and tentatively goes to the rear of the stage and inspects the ladder and paint cans. He returns with the stepladder. He puts it in position, facing the audience, next to The Painter's ladder.*)

THE MAN: Now what?

THE PAINTER: You need paint.

THE MAN: Sky blue?

THE PAINTER: If it suits you.

THE MAN: It does look nice.

THE PAINTER: Come on up, give it a try.

THE MAN: Well . . . Hmm.

> *(The Man returns upstage and retrieves a pair of clean white coveralls and a cap and puts them on. He picks up a paintbrush and examines it; he puts the brush into a pocket. He picks up a paint can and inspects it closely. Puts it down and picks up another paint can and inspects it.)*

THE MAN: *(Grinning.)* Sky blue.

> *(Paint can in hand, The Man climbs the ladder until he is side by side with The Painter. He puts the paint can on the ladder's shelf. The Man looks at The Painter and smiles. The Painter returns his smile. They both paint. Smiles beaming, they look at each other again, then continue painting. Joyfully, they break into song as they paint, perhaps a spirited rendition of a song appropriate to the title of this play.)*

(Curtain.)

END OF PLAY

PLEASE NOTE

Producers are hereby cautioned that permission to produce this play does not include permission to include any song under copyright.

Floored

GREGG KREUTZ

CHARACTERS

MITCH: somewhere between thirty and forty-five. Big, heavyset guy. Slow to burn but dangerous when pushed.

PHILIP: a little younger than Mitch. Good-looking charmer. Stronger on lively chat than self-preservation.

SETTING

A bare, windowless room

•   •   •

The set is a bare, windowless room, walls newly painted, and the floor just sanded. There is a closed door upstage center, and it is toward this door that Philip and Mitch are moving as they polyurethane the floor. Facing downstage, each armed with buckets and brushes, they are talking as they work. Philip, on the left side of the room attempts artistic finesse, Mitch, on the right, has a big man's plodding approach.

MITCH: Who cares?

PHILIP: Come on!

MITCH: Who cares?

PHILIP: How can you say that?! Aren't you even curious?!

MITCH: No. Who cares?

PHILIP: OK. OK. *You* don't. But for the moment pretend. For the hell of it. See if you can come up with an explanation.

MITCH: It's none of my business.

PHILIP: A plausible explanation. Alright? Try.

MITCH: No.

PHILIP: Come on.

MITCH: What's to explain? He needed his floor done. He met us. We're doing his floor.

PHILIP: Met us separately.

MITCH: Right.

PHILIP: Two strangers.

MITCH: Whatever.

PHILIP: Strangers to him and to each other.

MITCH: Is there some law you got to be intimate friends before you can apply varnish? Maybe we won't get caught.

PHILIP: Why would he hire two people who don't know each other and don't know anything about sanding and varnishing to sand and varnish?

MITCH: There isn't that much to know.

PHILIP: Yeah, well I don't think a sanding machine professional would gouge out all these ruts.

MITCH: They are not ruts.

PHILIP: OK, ravines. And look, you're supposed to apply the varnish *with* the grain. He's paying us a fortune, it wouldn't hurt to use the brush more sensitively.

MITCH: Hey, I'm doing the job, but I'm not gonna bust my chops being artistic.

PHILIP: For what Howard is paying you should be cutting off ears. I mean, man! How about that! All that money!

MITCH: What about it?

PHILIP: Why is it so much?! *(Pause.)* Huh?

MITCH: It isn't that much.

PHILIP: Come on; the guy is paying us a lot! You can get lawyers for less. Hell, for this much money you can get plumbers!

MITCH: He didn't want plumbers.

PHILIP: OK. See if you can explain this; Howard set up where to get the sanding machine, right? When I went to pick it up, I talked to the renter guy and he said they do sanding and varnishing. The renting company! The one Howard recommended.

MITCH: So?

PHILIP: So why didn't Howard use them?

MITCH: Too expensive.

PHILIP: No, that's what I'm telling you! I checked. They would do the whole job for a third of what we're getting. A third! And it would be a good job. Guaranteed ravine-free. So why us? *(Pause.)* Huh?

MITCH: Who cares?

PHILIP: Alright. Let's go at it from another direction. Let's break it down to components. Get a sense of who Howard is. How did you meet him?

MITCH: *(Wearily.)* I don't know.

PHILIP: Come on.

MITCH: Let's just finish the floor.

PHILIP: How'd you meet him?

MITCH: In this bar.

PHILIP: What kind of bar?

MITCH: Sports bar.

PHILIP: OK. See: We're starting to put together a composite, a profile. Putting the pieces together. Howard likes sports. And bars. So you two got to talking.

MITCH: Right.

PHILIP: Great! Now this is where I hope things jell. *(Significantly.)* Talking about what?

MITCH: Just talking.

PHILIP: Focus. Please. What was the topic?

MITCH: I don't know. Something. We both had a bet on the Giants. We lost money. We were commiserating.

PHILIP: And this was when?

MITCH: I told you. Two weeks ago. Sunday before last.

PHILIP: *(Pondering to himself.)* Two weeks ago. Two weeks ago. Hold it. Sensing discrepancy.

(Suddenly.)

AH HAH! I KNEW IT! I KNEW IT!

We have a breakthrough!

MITCH: What?

PHILIP: Giants *won* two weeks ago! 18 to 7. No commiserating. What'd you talk about?

MITCH: I tell you I really don't remember.

PHILIP: I get it! I get it! No problem, I'll go first. I understand. Howard is weird. He must have got you the way he got me: suckered into spilling your guts. Personal secrets. OK. No big deal. I'll tell you my big confession to Howard. I'll go first.

MITCH: Look, I don't . . .

PHILIP: Guess where I met him.

MITCH: Insane asylum.

PHILIP: Farmers Market. Union Square. That's where I work. Part-time. Selling produce.

MITCH: Figures.

PHILIP: I was pointing out to Howard how gorgeous the women at the market looked. Telling him how fresh fruit and vegetables seem to attract beauty.

MITCH: I hadn't heard.

PHILIP: Oh yeah. You lay out some apples or tomatoes or yams or carrots and you got yourself a lot of beautiful, sensuous women.

MITCH: Produce.

PHILIP: The more organically grown, the more gorgeous.

MITCH: Huh.

PHILIP: I'm sort of a free agent these days, romantically speaking, so I notice and as far as I'm concerned, forget about clubs or singles bars, if you want beautiful passionate women: Sell fruits and vegetables.

MITCH: I'm married.

PHILIP: So I'm pointing this out to Howard who I've just met and he's interested and all of a sudden he's got me describing this whole weird, personal situation I'm involved in. Out of the blue. Sort of unbelievably personal.

MITCH: Some kind of yam orgy?

PHILIP: No. This relationship. He got me talking about this tricky relationship. Kind of wild. It started a month ago, on this really freezing morning. During that cold snap. I was manning the stand. Vegetables laid out. Apples laid out. Mulled cider bubbling. I was in my lumber jack outfit. All the ingredients. You know, the trap was set. You can just feel the aura you pick up standing there. These gorgeous customers look on you like you're a hearty pioneer who's given his life over to apple farming.

MITCH: And *do* you live on a farm?

PHILIP: Naw. Twenty-eighth and Broadway. Walk-up. They just hired me to sell the apples. Normally I'm a musician. Sort of. So it was this icy morning and I notice a hauntingly beautiful woman standing there. Examining the Macintoshes. *(Pausing to look at the floor.)* By the way, this sheen is starting to look pretty good. It really pulls out the grain. Don't you think?

MITCH: *(Unenthusiastically.)* Yeah. Beautiful.

PHILIP: So I look at her, this woman, and figure: live one. We start talking. I run through my stuff; you know: Wine Sapp, Granny Smith, Ida red. Tart. Crisp. Everyone loves apple discussions. One thing leads to another and I end up saying, "Why don't you come back to my place and we can warm up?"

MITCH: Good one.

PHILIP: Well, good enough. I mean; we went. Everything was great. Actually amazing! Then the trouble started.

MITCH: She noticed it wasn't a farm.

PHILIP: No, she told me she was married.

MITCH: *(Suddenly frozen. Pause.)* Oh.

PHILIP: *(Downstage of Mitch and not noticing his changed demeanor.)* And what was bad was what she said about her husband.

MITCH: *(Resumes varnishing with a strange intensity.)* What about him?

PHILIP: It turned out he's kind of homicidally jealous.

MITCH: Yeah?

PHILIP: Violent. Viciously jealous. He's a bartender. Big, burly, you know. *(Mitch is making coarse strokes with his brush.)* Ham-fisted, tough, stocky, *(Mitch is jamming the brush into the can.)* insensitive. The more she talked about him the more unhappy I got. So I figured: Let's terminate this relationship.

MITCH: Oh.

PHILIP: But she kept coming back. Every market day; Monday, Wednesday, Friday, Saturday, Monday, Wednesday, Friday, Saturday, Monday, Wedn . . .

MITCH: *(Loud pain.)* OK!

PHILIP: You know, I wanted to end it . . .

MITCH: *(Wounded groan.)*

PHILIP: . . . but Hell, I'm human. What could I do? She was so beautiful and vulnerable and in love and said if I stopped seeing her she'd confess to her husband.

MITCH: *(Angry groan.)*

PHILIP: So that's the situation. Big-time dilemma. And that's what I told Howard about. The whole deal. I told him the story, I showed him her photograph. He got the full saga. I don't know why.

(Mitch, upstage of Philip has stopped varnishing.)

PHILIP: *(Continued.)* Howard just brought it out of me. So, what did you tell him?

(Pause.)

Huh? What did you talk to him about?

(Pause.)

Let's hear your big secret.

(Pause.)

Hey come on. Fair's fair.

(Pause.)

Alright, we'll go back; you were in this bar — sports bar — and you were talking and well OK, why did you and Howard start taking? What was the initial connection?

(Philip looks at Howard and sees he has stopped.)

Yeah. Take your time. Think back. What were you doing?

MITCH: *(Slowly.)* I was mixing him a Scotch and water. No ice.

PHILIP: Great. See. That's the idea. There you go. Now if we can just . . . Well now wait . . . You were mixing the . . . Getting the drink for . . . It's funny, I don't think that was clear before. That you *worked* in the Sports Bar. I thought you just *(Nervous laughter.)* were there. Patron. I've got to conjure up a different picture now. A different mental image. You're *behind* the bar. Yeah it's very different.

(False jolliness as he tries to quickly finish his side and get to the door.)

Well the main thing is we ended up, you and me, here however it happened. Howard met us and liked us and wanted to give us a little work and I see your point "Why read anything more into it." Exactly. God! Getting so convoluted and out of . . .

MITCH: *(Slowly with intensity.)* When I brought him the drink, Howard was staring at something on the wall behind me. Staring hard. Do you know what it was?

PHILIP: *(Thinly disguised nervousness.)* No. What was it?

MITCH: A picture.

PHILIP: I see.

MITCH: A picture of my wife.

PHILIP: Ah hah.

MITCH: I like to keep it hanging there above the cash register.

PHILIP: *(Trying to be upbeat.)* Good for you.

MITCH: He asked me about her. He said she looked familiar. I told him our relationship was having some trouble. Some trouble in the trust area.

PHILIP: You really don't need to go into any . . .

MITCH: When he finished his drink he laughed and offered me this job. I said sure. We shook hands.
(Pause.)
Howard laughs funny. I think he has a strange sense of humor.

PHILIP: *(By now, he and Mitch have backed themselves nearly up to the door.)* Look, I'm almost done. Virtually. Home stretch. In fact, could you do me a favor. Could you finish up this job. I'm sorry. I'm suddenly realizing that I'm — Damn, what is wrong with me? — I'm supposed to be at work. Like an hour ago!
(Reaching for the doorknob.)
I hate to abandon you but *(Struggling.)* I have completely lost track of the . . .
(The door won't open. Trying to smile.)
Isn't that funny; Howard seems to have locked the door.
(Blackout.)

END OF PLAY

Partridge in a Pear Tree

FREDERICK STROPPEL

Partridge in a Pear Tree was first staged at the Nuyorican Poets Café in N.Y.C. It was directed by the author, with the following cast: Scott — Peter Plano; Murph — Kevin Kash.

CHARACTERS
SCOTT
MURPH

SETTING
A room in Scott's house

. . .

A Christmas party. Murph is at the buffet table, picking at various appetizers, a plastic cup of eggnog in his hand. Scott, the host, wearing a bright-red Christmas sweater, approaches with two cups in his hand. He's a little tipsy, in a jolly way.

SCOTT: Hey, Murph. I got you an eggnog.

MURPH: I already have one.

SCOTT: Now you have two. Can't fly on one wing.

MURPH: *(Takes the cup.)* It's your party, Scott, I'm not gonna argue with you.

SCOTT: Merry Christmas!

MURPH: Feliz Navidad.

(They drink.)

SCOTT: *(Points to his lip.)* Look. Eggnog moustache. "Got nog?"
(Chuckles to himself.)
So, you're enjoying yourself, I hope?

MURPH: Great appetizers. I'm loving these cheese things.

SCOTT: Oh, yeah, Gloria's famous Christmas cheese balls. It's, what? — cheddar cheese, crumbled Jimmy Dean sausage, Bisquick . . . She's an amazing cook.

MURPH: She made all this stuff?

SCOTT: Well, some of it's from Costco, but — she put it all in the oven. She's a wiz.

MURPH: You know what's good? Swedish meatballs.

SCOTT: I don't think we have Swedish meatballs.

MURPH: You might want to think about it for next year. A sure crowd-pleaser.

SCOTT: Well, we've been having this party for seventeen years now, we have our menu pretty much figured out. Every now and then we try something new — like last year, we added the little mini-quiches — but for the most part, we stick to the tried-and-true. The shrimp tree, the famous eggnog . . . Why tinker with success? Christmas is all about tradition.

MURPH: *(Points.)* I hope *that's* a new tradition.

SCOTT: What?

MURPH: That cute little Santa's Helper over there, in the green tights. She can help me anytime.

SCOTT: That's my daughter.

MURPH: Really? That's . . . ?

(Tries to remember.)

SCOTT: Megan.

MURPH: That's Megan? Wow. She got — big.

SCOTT: They grow up fast. How are your kids?

MURPH: I don't know. Joanne took them out to Ohio with her, trying to keep me away from them. Like I'm a bad influence or something.

SCOTT: She won't let you see them?

MURPH: She'll let me see them if I go out to fucking Ohio, but that's not gonna happen. She's turned them all against me, anyway. Not one Christmas card this year.

SCOTT: That's a shame. And you sent them all cards?

MURPH: I don't have time for that. I'm up to my ears in work.

SCOTT: You still at the car wash?

MURPH: I'm the manager now.

SCOTT: Wow — congratulations.

MURPH: It just means twice as much work. Look at my hands. That's from all that industrial detergent. I should be getting compensation. Who knows what kind of chemicals I got inside me? I could be growing tumors as we speak. Plus these nitwits I got working for me, most of them are from Guatemala or somewhere, they've never even *seen* a car.

(Makes a circular motion with his hand.)

I tell them, concentric circles, concentric circles . . . ! In one ear and out their ass, you know? And then the customer tips me five bucks and says split it up. With four other guys? That's like a dollar each. They'd just spend it all on Heineken or Thunderbird anyway.

SCOTT: So you keep the money yourself?

MURPH: It goes to a favorite charity.

(Beat.)

So how old is she?

SCOTT: Who?

MURPH: Megan.

SCOTT: Fifteen.

MURPH: Fifteen! Going on twenty-eight, huh?

SCOTT: She's very mature for her age. You know, she's the only sophomore on the varsity lacrosse team. Straight-A student. She works weekends at Annie Sez, and she does babysitting on the side. And she's the president of her French club.

MURPH: French, huh?

SCOTT: But she still has time for her family. That's the great thing. She passed up a big ski trip with the cheerleading squad to be here tonight. "Oh no, Daddy, I couldn't miss the Christmas party."

MURPH: God bless her.

SCOTT: She's a special kid. We're very proud of her.

MURPH: I would think so.

SCOTT: I'm a lucky, lucky man.

(Shakes head.)

And I think I'm getting a little buzzed.

MURPH: You're not used to it. I could drink all day, it doesn't affect me.

SCOTT: I know I'm sounding like a big cornball, but God, I just love Christmas. The songs, and the lights, even the shopping. The hustle and bustle, there's just nothing like it. Everyone's friendlier, there's a spirit of good will in the air.

(Sings.)

"It's the most wonderful time of the year . . . !" And when you've got your family around you — sitting around the fireplace, telling stories, singing songs — that's what it's all about.

MURPH: *(To himself.)* Fifteen . . . !

SCOTT: What are you doing for Christmas, Murph?

MURPH: Ahh, the usual. Get some takeout from Boston Market. Maybe head down to the Dribble Inn for a few drinks. Just another day.

SCOTT: You wanna come over here?

MURPH: For Christmas? Oh, I don't know . . .

SCOTT: Why not? We're gonna have a big Christmas dinner, there'll be plenty of food — I'll tell Gloria to make you those Swedish meatballs. You don't want to be alone on Christmas Day.

MURPH: I probably should visit my parents. They're gonna be wondering where I am.

SCOTT: All right, well, come over Christmas Eve. We can all go to Midnight Mass together. Megan is singing in the choir.

MURPH: She is?

SCOTT: Sure, it'll be great. You know, church on Christmas Eve — that's the ultimate, you know? The whole spiritual aspect of the season really hits you. Because that's what it's all about, I don't care what anybody says. This bullshit about "Happy Holidays" . . . It really sticks in my craw. Somebody says "Happy Holidays" to me, I say right back, "Merry Christmas! *Merry Christmas!*" And if they've got a problem with that, too bad. You have to stand tall for your faith.

MURPH: Is she gonna be wearing that outfit?

SCOTT: Who?

MURPH: Megan. On Christmas Eve.

SCOTT: No, it's a High Mass. She can't be dressed like an elf.

MURPH: That's too bad, because she looks amazing in it. I can't believe she's fifteen.

SCOTT: What do you mean?

MURPH: I mean, she's very attractive. *Very* attractive.

SCOTT: Yeah, she's a pretty girl.

MURPH: Come on, she's fucking gorgeous. She looks like that whatsherface, Scarlett Johansson. Man, there's another one I wouldn't mind slipping the old yule log.

SCOTT: Getting back to Christmas Eve . . .

MURPH: I mean, no offense, but it's hard to believe she's related to you. Because let's face it, you're an ugly fuck.

SCOTT: I guess she takes after her mom.

MURPH: Yeah, that's true — I always thought Gloria was pretty hot. And I mean that in the most respectful way.

SCOTT: *(Checks his watch.)* Hey, I think it's time we started caroling . . .

MURPH: I don't envy you, man, you're gonna have your hands full with her. You gotta believe every guy in school is gonna be looking to bang her.

SCOTT: What?

MURPH: You know what high school kids are like. All hopped up on hormones. And you said she's a cheerleader? Jesus Christ, that's like waving a red carrot in front of those football players. Plus you got all those male cheerleaders, too, staring up her dress while she's shaking her pom-poms. I mean, I don't care how gay they are, there has to be some subterranean appreciation going on there.

SCOTT: I'm not worried about Megan. She's a very sensible girl.

MURPH: *(Scoffs.)* Yeah, right. Like you have any idea what kids are up to these days. They got the Internet, and all the crap on cable TV, and a hundred different kinds of condoms. She may act like Miss Innocent, but you can bet your ass she knows what's going on. Especially with that body.

SCOTT: I really don't think we should talk about this anymore . . .

MURPH: I'm just offering you a clear-eyed perspective on the situation. I know it's upsetting to think of your daughter doing the deed, but you gotta face reality.

SCOTT: Murph, she's only fifteen.

MURPH: So was Lori Schneider, but that didn't stop you from banging her under the bleachers, remember, after the Rangers won the Cup? And she wasn't half as foxy as your daughter. Frankly, I wouldn't have even let that pig give me a hand job, but you were in a celebratory mood, and that's how things happen. Hormones. You gotta keep an eye on her, I'm telling you. That's trouble waiting to happen.

SCOTT: Uh . . . Excuse me, Murph, I think I'd better go talk to some of the other guests . . .

MURPH: Yeah, sure, fulfill your hosting duties, I'll just stay right here and enjoy the view.

SCOTT: What view?

MURPH: You know, the general atmosphere. Hey — do you have any mistletoe?

SCOTT: Mistletoe?

MURPH: It's a festive touch for the holiday season. Remember that party at Dave Hubble's house, when his mom was drunk, and she was grabbing us all under the mistletoe? She was a horny old bitch, she had these wet slobbery lips, and we were all trying to avoid her, but I took the opposite tack, I said, "Hey, she wants some action, I'll give her some action," so when she grabbed me, I grabbed right back, got me a handful of tit, stuck my tongue right down her throat. Gave her a full tonsil massage.
(Laughs.)
That sobered her right up, let me tell you.

SCOTT: That's a great story, but really not appropriate to this setting . . .

MURPH: See, when I was young I used to do these lingual exercises I found in a magazine. My tongue is a skilled and flexible instrument.
(Beat.)

SCOTT: No, we don't have any mistletoe.

MURPH: Too bad. Gotta say, this eggnog is making me a little frisky. Probably the egg element — fertility, and all that.

SCOTT: Maybe you'd better slow down a little.

MURPH: I'm fine. Worse comes to worst, I can crash on your couch.

SCOTT: No, but I mean, this is a family Christmas party, you don't want to do something embarrassing.

MURPH: Nothing embarrasses me. You're the one who should slow down, with a daughter like that.

SCOTT: What do you mean?

MURPH: I mean, you got something like that bouncing around the house all the time, it's bound to cause stress. And then you have a couple of drinks, and things happen.

SCOTT: What are you talking about?

MURPH: Hey, I know how it is. My sister, Tracy — you remember her? She used to walk around the house in her underwear, sometimes just a thong, and you wouldn't be human if that didn't turn you on. Not that I ever acted on my impulses — there was no penetration or anything — but we had some intense wrestling matches.

SCOTT: All right, Murph, you know what? — enough. You're really crossing the line now.

MURPH: What do you mean?

SCOTT: I mean, I don't want to hear any more talk about Megan. That's it!

MURPH: Who's talking about Megan? I'm talking about my sister.

SCOTT: Well, I don't want to hear about your trampy sister, either, OK? This is a Christmas party. Let's talk about Christmasy things, all right? I mean . . . Jesus Christ!

MURPH: I sense that you're uncomfortable with this subject. Are my comments cutting too close to your bone?

SCOTT: Your comments are ridiculous! I don't know what goes on in your world, but around here we go to church and we eat cheese balls, and we don't lust after our own children!

MURPH: Not for nothing, Scott, but you're living in a bubble. I mean, you're up there in your office in the clouds, trading stock options or whatever the fuck you do, and I'm down on the street, in the real world, washing cars. I know what people are capable of, and it's not pretty.

SCOTT: Well, *I'm* not capable of it, and nobody I know is capable of it, except maybe *you*.

MURPH: Don't sell yourself short. We're all members of the human family. And sometimes families get a little crazy. Like, she comes skipping home from school with her report card, you give her a big hug, you feel her pressing her perky you-know-whats against you, and next thing you know you're off to the races. And what I'm saying is, you shouldn't be ashamed of that. It's a natural thing and in many ways a healthy thing. As long as you *channel* it. You know, redirect it toward your wife, or a hooker or something. Give Lori Schneider a call. 'Cause you really don't want to bang your daughter if you can possibly avoid it.

SCOTT: *(Had enough.)* All right, get out.

MURPH: What?

SCOTT: Get out. I want you to go home.

MURPH: Why?

SCOTT: Because the party's over.

MURPH: We didn't even carol yet.

SCOTT: You can carol to yourself on the way out. You're leaving.

MURPH: Something I said?

SCOTT: You know, Murph, I invite you to my party every year because I've known you since high school, and it seems like, with the holiday season and the end of the year upon us, it's the perfect time to reach out and renew old ties. But the fact is, over the years we've grown apart: I'm a normal decent person, and you're a sick fuck. Every year you come here, you show up half-drunk, you wind up spouting a lot of stupid shit, which I try to overlook because it's in the spirit of Christ to forgive, but this is the limit, I can't take it anymore. I mean, what the fuck is wrong with you? It's Christmas! You don't talk about sex at Christmas!

MURPH: Did I mention the word *sex?* I don't think so.

SCOTT: No, you said "banging," which is so much less offensive, but it amounts to the same thing. You're standing here suggesting that I might sleep with my own daughter, which is the most disgusting, outrageous . . . ! I'm running out of words.

MURPH: *(Helpfully.)* Perverted?

SCOTT: What makes you even think this way? You have kids of your own.

MURPH: Yeah, but they're in Ohio.

SCOTT: Lucky for them, huh?

MURPH: So you mean to say you never had an impure thought about her? *Never?*

SCOTT: No, never!

MURPH: Not even once?

SCOTT: She's my daughter!

MURPH: Like maybe once you might have forgotten who she was, and you saw her from behind, and you got a little momentary elevation . . . ?
(Scott just glares at him.)
Well, then you're a better man than I am, and I salute you. Because if she was *my* daughter, I can tell you right now . . .

SCOTT: Murph, you have to shut up, right now . . .

MURPH: I'm just saying . . .

SCOTT: Stop talking, will you?

MURPH: As a member of the human family . . .

SCOTT: WILL YOU SHUT THE FUCK UP? I swear to you, if you so much as touch her, I will cut your hands off, I will cut your dick off, I will tear you limb from limb with my bare hands . . . !

MURPH: Whoa, whoa! What happened to your Christmas spirit? Don't you see what you're doing here? You're projecting your forbidden desires onto me. What do I care about Megan? She's fucking fifteen! That'll be the day, when I start hitting on my friend's kids. *That's* sick.

(Beat, as Scott pulls himself together.)

SCOTT: Just go, will you? Just *go.*

MURPH: OK, I'm going. I'll see you on Christmas Eve.

SCOTT: No — I don't think so.

MURPH: Oh, so now you're rescinding your invitation? That's great. Mr. Christmas. OK, fine, I can find the church by myself.

SCOTT: I doubt it.

MURPH: This is a bullshit party anyway. Like I have nothing better to do but sing a bunch of fucking carols all night.

(He heads for the door.)

I'll get my own coat. You stay here and eat your quiches and wear your dopey sweater and pretend that you're some kind of fucking saint. But I know people, and I know *you.*

(Murph exits. Scott has to take a moment to regain his composure. Just when he's ready to get back in party mode, Murph pops his head back in.)

MURPH: Hey, Scott —

SCOTT: Yeah?

MURPH: Happy Holidays.

SCOTT: Fuck you!

(But Murph is already gone.)

END OF PLAY

The Duel

A retelling of Pushkin's Eugene Onegin

JEFF TABNICK

CHARACTERS
    EUGENE: mid-late twenties
    VLADIMIR: mid-late twenties

TIME
    First half of the nineteenth century

SETTING
    Russian steppe

•   •   •

Empty stage. Eugene enters from one side of the stage. Vladimir enters from the other. They both hold pistols at their sides.

EUGENE: Vladimir, you're a fucking idiot.
VLADIMIR: I'm a fucking idiot?
    (As he polishes his gun.)
    Oh I'm a fucking idiot. I'm a fucking idiot? *I'm* a fucking idiot?
EUGENE: Yes.
VLADIMIR: Yes I'm a fucking idiot. Everyone knows that I'm a fucking idiot.
EUGENE: Does Olga know?
VLADIMIR: That I'm a fucking idiot?
EUGENE: That you're a fucking idiot.
VLADIMIR: She doesn't know that I'm a fucking idiot.
EUGENE: Does she know where you are at this ungodly morning hour?
VLADIMIR: No.
EUGENE: If she did, she too, would know that you are a fucking idiot.
VLADIMIR: I could gain three hundred pounds and stroll down Nevsky Prospect in my underwear while farting "The Marseillaise" and still Olga wouldn't know that I'm a fucking idiot. Such are women.
EUGENE: Of a certain type.
    (Beat.)
EUGENE: Look, call off this duel, go home to her. You can't afford to lose her. Because most women know that you *are* a fucking idiot.
VLADIMIR: Yes *now*. After what, what a. What a.
EUGENE: What a what?
VLADIMIR: You're the reason everyone knows that I'm a fucking idiot —
EUGENE: You're making too much of that.
VLADIMIR: Am I? Tell me, tell me — tell me.

EUGENE: What?

VLADIMIR: That not everyone is laughing at me?

EUGENE: How would I know? It's not like I hang out with them, it's not like they're my *buddies*. These landowners and old people with their sticky mucus children.

(*Suddenly irritated.*)

I didn't want to go to Tatiana Larin's fucking name day party in the first place.

VLADIMIR: Eugene, I invited you, you said yes.

EUGENE: You told me that it would be an intimate gathering of young intellectuals.

VLADIMIR: I don't remember saying that.

EUGENE: Instead there were droshkies lined up four versts —

VLADIMIR: Fine.

EUGENE: (*Continuous.*) — down the road.

VLADIMIR: And all of that.

EUGENE: (*Continuous.*) And I walk in and it's a name day party — all of these fat families eating and eating and eating.

VLADIMIR: They weren't all fat.

EUGENE: Vulgar! Vulgar!

EUGENE: Gvozdin a *fat* farmer (yet at least ten of his serfs die of hunger each year), the hunchbacked Skotinins who look more like siblings than husband and wife . . .

VLADIMIR: They're —

EUGENE: (*Continuous.*) . . . Petushkov, that gray-haired fop who falls all over himself to make those other idiots laugh . . .

VLADIMIR: I get it —

EUGENE: Flyanov the usurer, Kharlivkov the cuckold *five* times over —

VLADIMIR: I get it, dear lord, I get it!

EUGENE: And the young major with the protruding veins who flirts with the old women because the young ones won't look at him.

VLADIMIR: I get it!

EUGENE: You know how I feel about adult parties.

VLADIMIR: *I* thought —

EUGENE: They make me irritable. It is *I* that should be challenging *you* to a duel!

VLADIMIR: Because adult parties make you irritable?

EUGENE: And once I am irritable there is no telling what I will do! I am simply spoilt, that's all.

VLADIMIR: *You* have no need to challenge *me* to a duel, you've already dealt me a fatal blow.

EUGENE: Good then there is no need for me to deal you another one, simply redundant, in fact impossible to deal one person two fatal blows.

VLADIMIR: Stop this. Let's be clear. We are here —

EUGENE: Oh I know why —

VLADIMIR: I'm sure you do.

EUGENE: I do.

VLADIMIR: I need to say it for the sake of our seconds who stand there and there.

EUGENE: Oh they *know* why —

VLADIMIR: I have challenged you to a duel because at Tatiana Larin's name day party, you danced the mazurka with Olga my bride-to-be not one time but two times. And then when I asked my bride-to-be to dance the last cotillion with me, she got all flushed in the face and apologized and said no, because you'd already asked her to dance the last cotillion with you, and she felt she couldn't say no to you, you being my dear dear friend. And then I and the rest of the party watched you dance with her and squeeze her hand and whisper in her ear and make other . . . lascivious advances toward her. You *soiled* the good name of the cotillion.

EUGENE: Do you think *she* fancies *me*?

VLADIMIR: No. Of course not. God forbid!

EUGENE: Pity, I was thinking of paying her a visit after I'm done with you.

(Vladimir raises his gun.)

EUGENE: Oh I'm just having at you, I am fooling, just like I was that night. Trying to get a rise out of you. It's too tempting, you take yourself far too seriously.

VLADIMIR: Eugene — . We're not. We are not. Twenty-two anymore. This isn't games. That is all I've been trying —

EUGENE: See here.

(With sudden fury.)

That is why you tricked me into going to Tatiana Larin's infernal name day party! Isn't it? Isn't it? You know that I love you and would not do anything to shame you but you really really pushed me to it.

VLADIMIR: By inviting you to a party?

EUGENE: After all of the. Do you.

(Sincerely asking.)

Do you really not know me better than that?

VLADIMIR: I thought you were changing.

EUGENE: You are the one who has changed. Remember in Petersburg? The nights at the opera. In the stalls. Hissing and booing and using our glasses to peer at the young women in the tiers?

VLADIMIR: Of course I do.

EUGENE: Dashing from one party to the next. Making fun of the guests. Flirting with the girls and breaking their hearts.

VLADIMIR: Yes.

EUGENE: Drinking ourselves silly.

VLADIMIR: Eugene —

EUGENE: Having lofty conversations about. Socialism —

VLADIMIR: Of course.

EUGENE: *(Continuous.)* — while walking along the Neva. Discussing Saint Simon. Espousing his ideals. And then when my uncle that old fart went and died and left me his cottage, I moved up here, to take a time out from city life — *just* a time out — detox. And you moved close by, to your family's property — I thought that is a friend!

VLADIMIR: I needed some detox too.

EUGENE: He needs me.

EUGENE: And the nights reading and writing poetry. Waking at noon. And shooting partridges and dining together, and I was enjoying this life so much I even put up with your constant talk about. Olga.

VLADIMIR: I don't know what that has to do with —

EUGENE: And still you think I'd be interested in that party — I thought you alone knew me.

VLADIMIR: I thought you would be interested in Tatiana Larin, maybe even interested enough to —

EUGENE: She's a pretty girl. But I know what will happen, I will have at her and then I will be bored of her and then I will hurt her. What am I supposed to do? Marry her?

VLADIMIR: Yes! Exactly.

EUGENE: *(Continuous.)* Spend all my time with her infernal fat family and add to it with even more fat brats?

VLADIMIR: That is what I intend to do with Olga.

(Eugene impulsively raises his gun but then stops himself. He collects himself. He says . . .)

EUGENE: Look, let's go home. Before I become irritable again. Call off this duel.

VLADIMIR: You insulted me in front of my future life!

EUGENE: As soon as Andrei the holy fool masturbates in public again, they'll forget it, on to the next scandal.

VLADIMIR: And you were supposed to be my friend.

EUGENE: You were supposed to be mine.

VLADIMIR: I didn't shame you in public.

EUGENE: No, your offense was much more private.

(Beat.)

VLADIMIR: To be talked out of a duel would be —

EUGENE: I won't tell anyone —

VLADIMIR: Maybe we could — But our seconds will tell! And then everyone will know not only can Eugene dance with my wife, but he can also talk me out of a duel. I'm your inferior, your pushover, your lackey. I don't deny in some ways that has always been true.

EUGENE: I deny it.

VLADIMIR: I can't appear that way in Olga's eyes.

(Beat.)

It's impossible to call it off now anyway! Serfs are even gathering. It's time to think about more serious things Eugene.

EUGENE: What's serious, all of the sudden your reputation is serious?

VLADIMIR: I mean can you really go around aimlessly every day, reading and hunting and — ?

EUGENE: Yes I can.

VLADIMIR: Without anyone special to share it with?

(Eugene is silent.)

VLADIMIR: But *I'm* getting married!

(Beat.)

And all this time I thought it was I who needed you.

(Beat.)

Take Tatiana! She is a fine woman, she would never even deign to look upon me — Only *you* could have her!

EUGENE: (Suddenly hopeful.) You think she is pretty?

VLADIMIR: She is the most beautiful woman in this village.

EUGENE: Then you shouldn't settle for Olga, my friend, I will help you plot to win over Tatiana!

VLADIMIR: Eugene.

EUGENE: You just said Tatiana is prettier — we will perform this play together.

VLADIMIR: I am marrying Olga. And we are moving far away from here.

(Beat.)

EUGENE: Moving away? Where? To Petersburg, well fine, we can all three of us go back to Peter, if that's how it has to be.

VLADIMIR: I can't have you around her.

EUGENE: You mean you're moving away from *me?*

VLADIMIR: Yes.

EUGENE: You wouldn't.

EUGENE: You've given me no choice.

EUGENE: It was a joke!

VLADIMIR: I don't trust you anymore, Eugene.

> *(Beat.)*

EUGENE: On my part anyway.

VLADIMIR: What does that mean?

EUGENE: It's not *my* trust you should doubt.

> *(Eugene's attitude is suddenly darker, unforgiving.)*

EUGENE: Admittedly, I asked Olga to dance the mazurka to have my revenge on you for taking me to that infernal party, but *she* asked *me* to dance the last cotillion.

VLADIMIR: A lie!

EUGENE: You'll never know for sure.

VLADIMIR: I have faith in *Olga.*

EUGENE: What are you putting your faith in? The false moniker of love? She would have taken anyone who floated down the river into lake Olga — there are no dams to keep the riffraff out of lake Olga — and there is your precious love. Anyone who would take her, that is her definition of love and I know because I took her. How can you possibly marry her now?

VLADIMIR: I love her.

EUGENE: *What?* Can I talk no sense to you, man? *That* is your love? That! Not shared interests, or intellectual fervor, or adventure! A weak reliance on a cow-eyed baby machine!

VLADIMIR: You child.

EUGENE: If I killed you, it would be a mercy killing.

VLADIMIR: *You* are the fucking idiot.

EUGENE: Ah.

VLADIMIR: It is time for you to grow up.

EUGENE: Never.

VLADIMIR: Then ten paces.

EUGENE: With pleasure.

> *(They line up back-to-back and walk ten paces, but must still remain on stage. They aim their guns. Vladimir fires. He misses but he was clearly trying to kill Eugene.)*

EUGENE: You shot at me!

VLADIMIR: It's a duel.

EUGENE: But you. Shot. *At.* Me. I was going to shoot at that tree, or at the sky, but you, you, you really wanted to kill me.

VLADIMIR: Eugene —

EUGENE: Don't move, I haven't taken my shot yet.

VLADIMIR: *(Frightened.)* I know that, of course, perfectly within your rights, of course, but. Buddy. Buddy. I think you see. I didn't actually hit you, by the way, just to the right, *just*, that was planned. I was just trying to convince you that, that things are more serious now, we need to grow up —

(Eugene shoots Vladimir. Vladimir falls. Eugene walks over to him, feels for his pulse. He is dead.)

EUGENE: I'm convinced.

(Blackout.)

END OF PLAY

Black Paintings © 2005 by Neil Olson. Reprinted by permission of the author. For performance rights, contact Donadio and Olson, Inc., 121 W. 27th St. #704, New York, NY 10001-6207.

Blue in the Face © 2007 by Kayla Cagan. Reprinted by permission of the author. For performance rights, contact Smith and Kraus, Inc. (Web site: www.smithandkraus.com) e-mail: sandk@sover.net

Blue Skies © 2007 by Marvin L. Cotlar. Reprinted by permission of the author. For performance rights, contact the author: mlcotlar@mweb.co.cw

Bone China © 2007 by K. Alexa Mavromatis. Reprinted by permission of the author. For performance rights, contact Smith and Kraus, Inc. (Web site: www.smithandkraus.com) e-mail: sandk@sover.net

Don't Listen to What It Sounds Like © 2007 by Mark Borkowski. Reprinted by permission of the author. For performance rights, contact the author: mborkowski@aol.com

Double D © 2004 by Jim Dalglish. Reprinted by permission of the author. For performance rights, contact Smith and Kraus, Inc. (Web site: www.smithandkraus.com) e-mail: sandk@sover.net

The Duel © 2006 by Jeff Tabnick. Reprinted by permission of the author. For performance rights, contact the author: jefftabnick@yahoo.com

The 11:05 © 2007 by Liz Amberly. Reprinted by permission of the author. For performance rights, contact the author: lizamberly@mac.com

Floored © 2007 by Gregg Kreutz. Reprinted by permission of the author. For performance rights, contact Smith and Kraus, Inc. (Web site: www.smithandkraus.com) e-mail: sandk@sover.net

An Honest Arrangement © 2005 by David Wiener. Reprinted by permission of the author. For performance rights, contact the author: dwiener@ucsd.edu

Horticultural Therapy © 2007 by George Sauer. Reprinted by permission of the author. For performance rights, contact Smith and Kraus, Inc. (Web site: www.smithandkraus.com) e-mail: sandk@sover.net

If I Could Paint the Rain © 2007 by Rosary O'Neill. Reprinted by permission of Tonda Marton, The Marton Agency, 1 Union Sq. W. #813, New York, NY 10003. For performance rights, contact Tonda Marton (tonda@martonagency.com) 212-255-1908.